Baroque Music for Clarinet

Dr. Norman Heim

PIANO ACCOMPANIMENT

MEL BAY

Visit us at www.melbay.com — E-mail us at email@melbay.com

Preface

This collection of Baroque music is arranged for the intermediate level clarinetist with the piano part being of equal skill level. The music is taken from keyboard, song and chamber music sources and represents quality Baroque styles circa 1625 – 1775. This music can be played by clarinetists for church, festival, school and leisure occasions.

Dr. Norman Heim
Gaithersburg, Maryland

Table of Contents

Arioso

Johann S. Bach
(1685-1750)

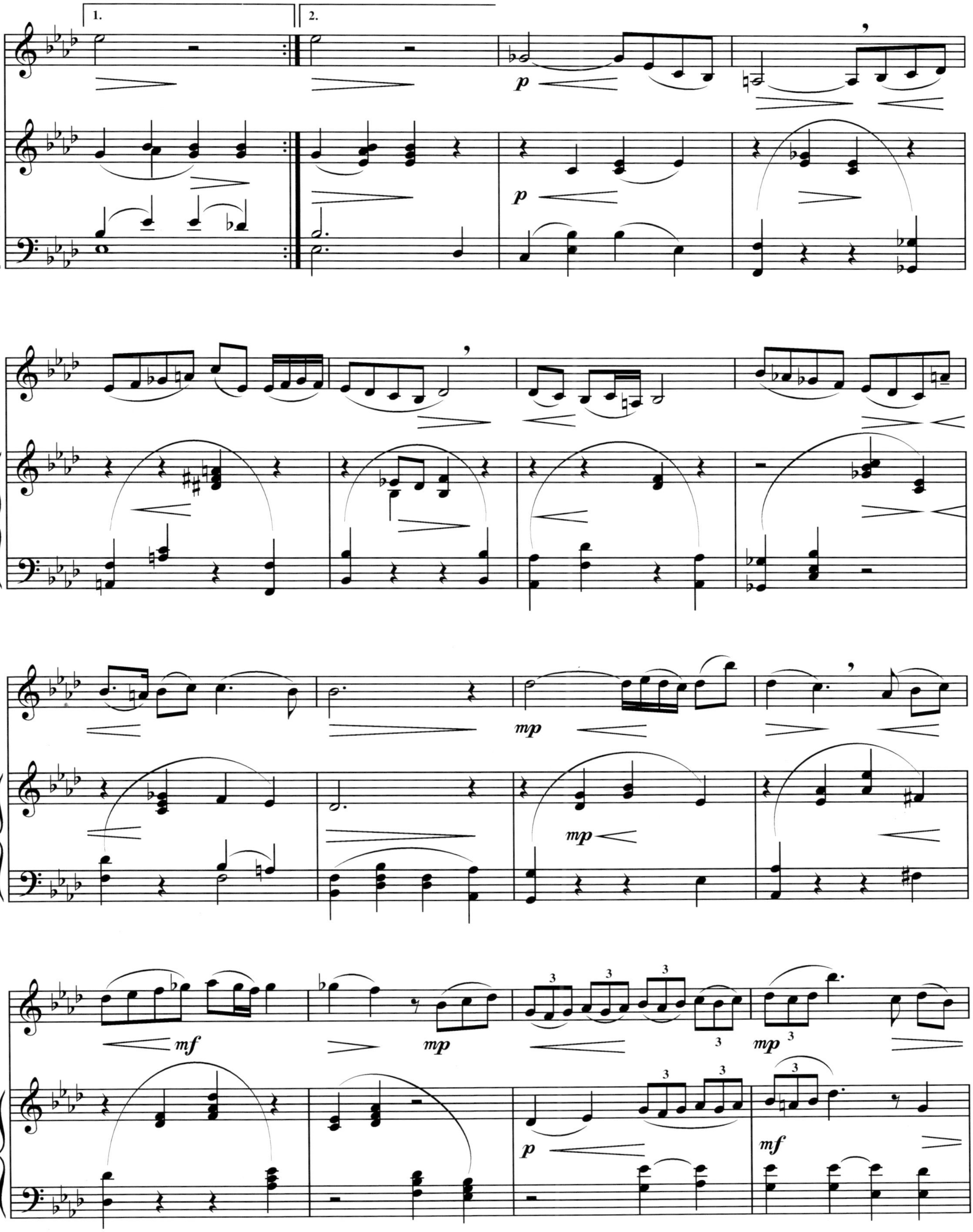
1.
2.
p
mp
mf

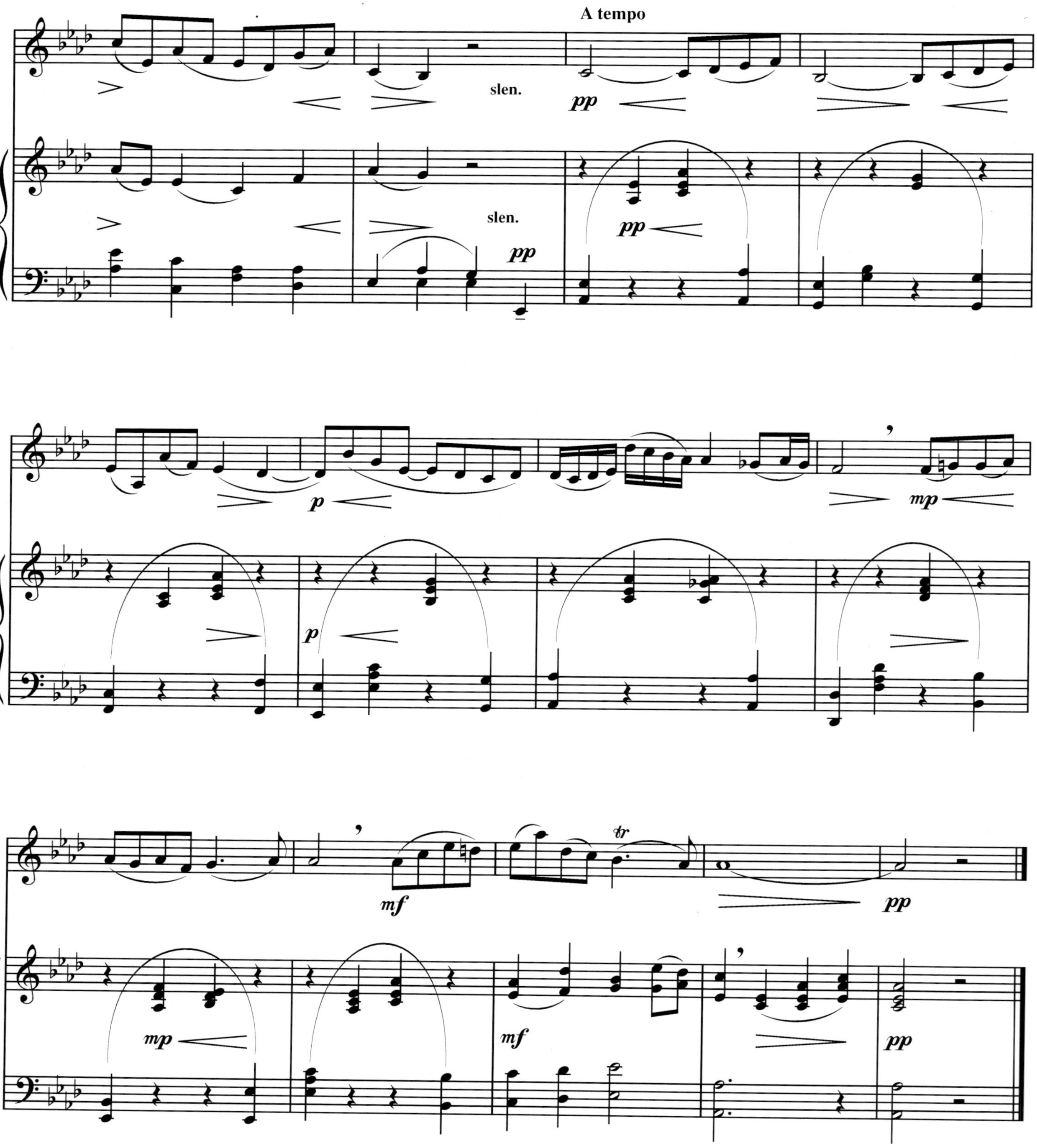
A tempo
slen.
pp
slen.
pp
pp
p
p
mp
mp
mf
tr
mf
pp
pp

Le Tambourin
(The Drummer)

Jean P. Rameau
(1683-1764)

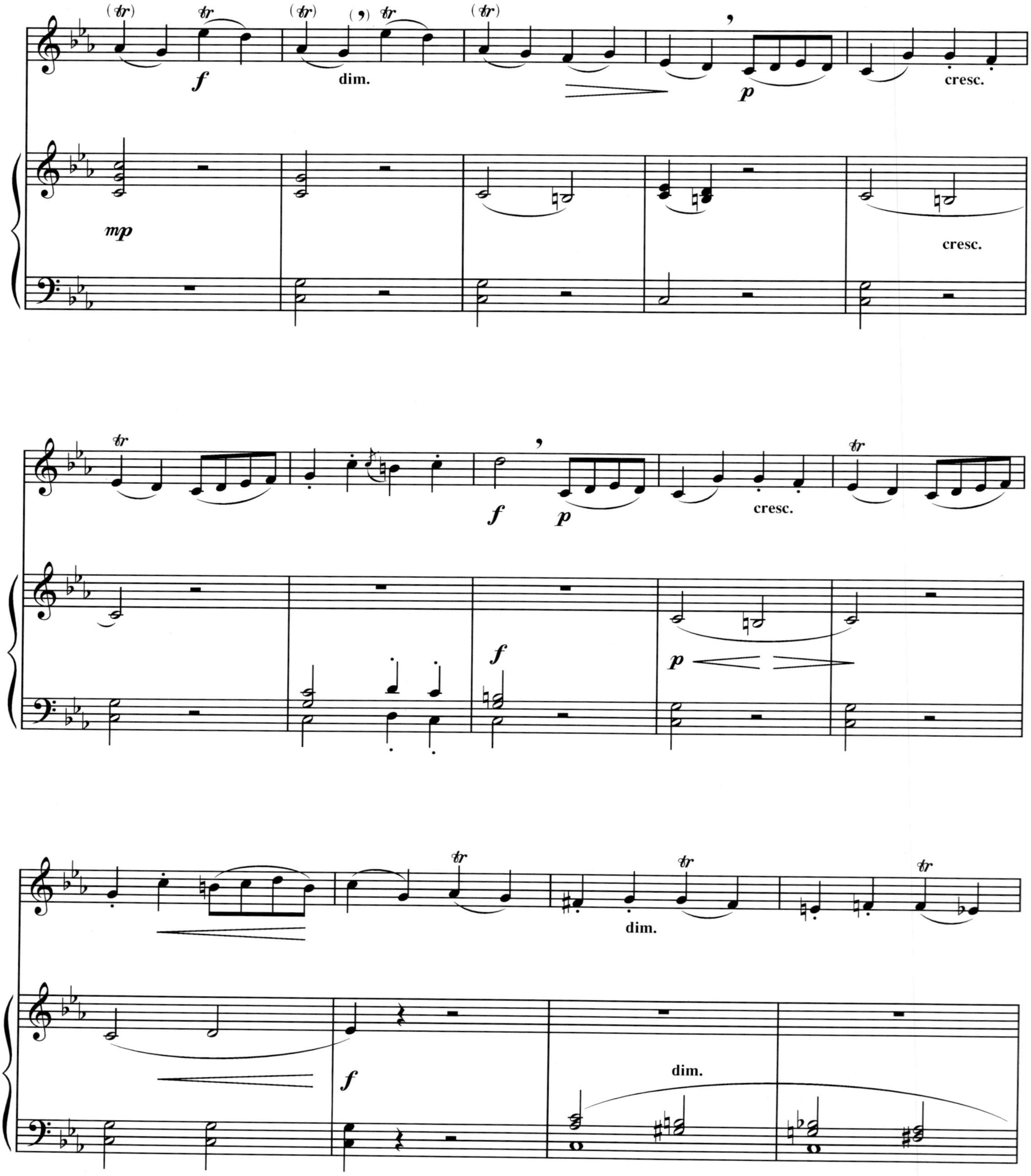
(tr)
tr
f
dim.
p
cresc.
mp

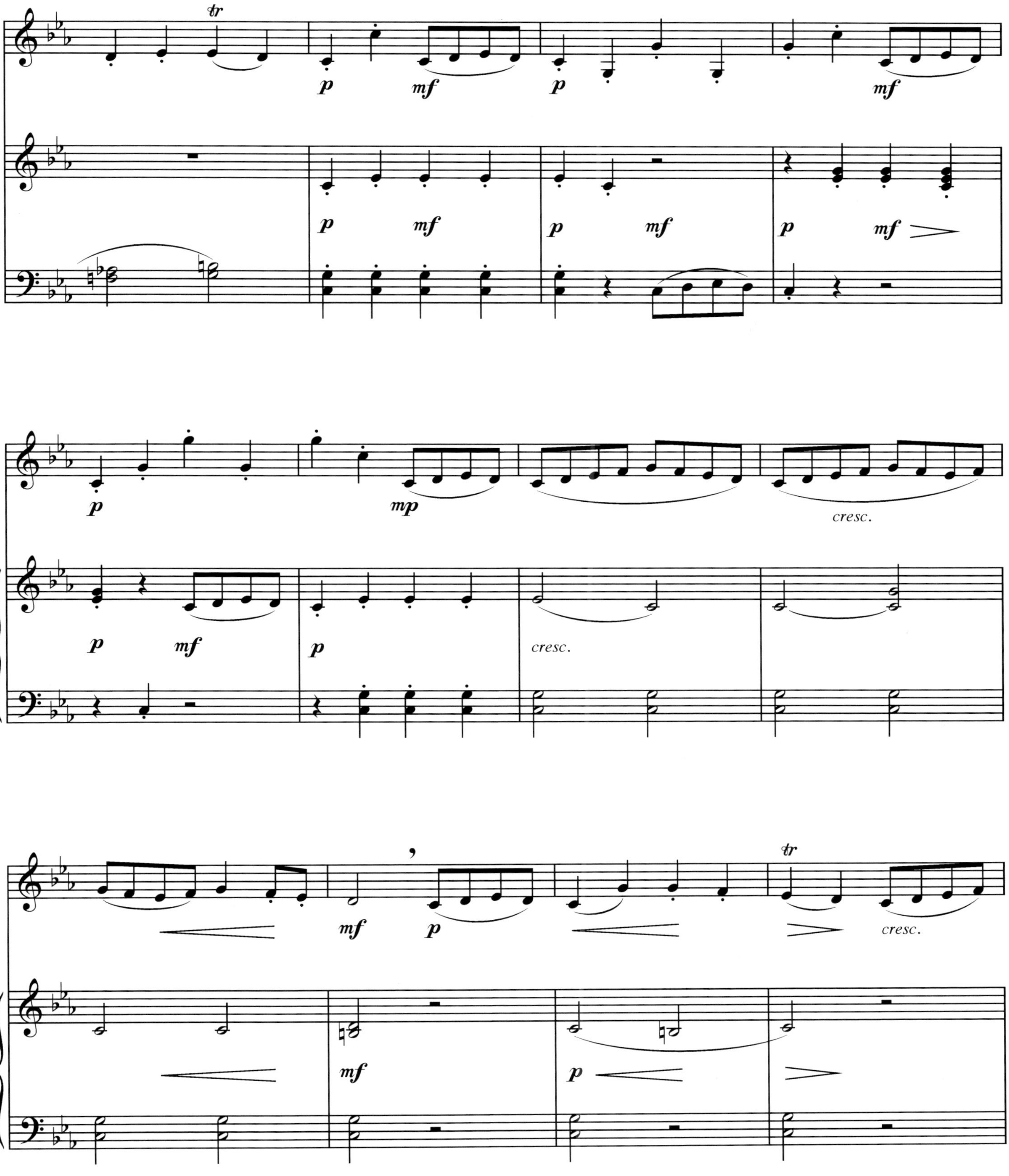
tr
p
mf
p
mf
p
mf
p
mf
p
mf
p
mp
p
mf
p
cresc.
cresc.
tr
mf
p
cresc.
mf
p

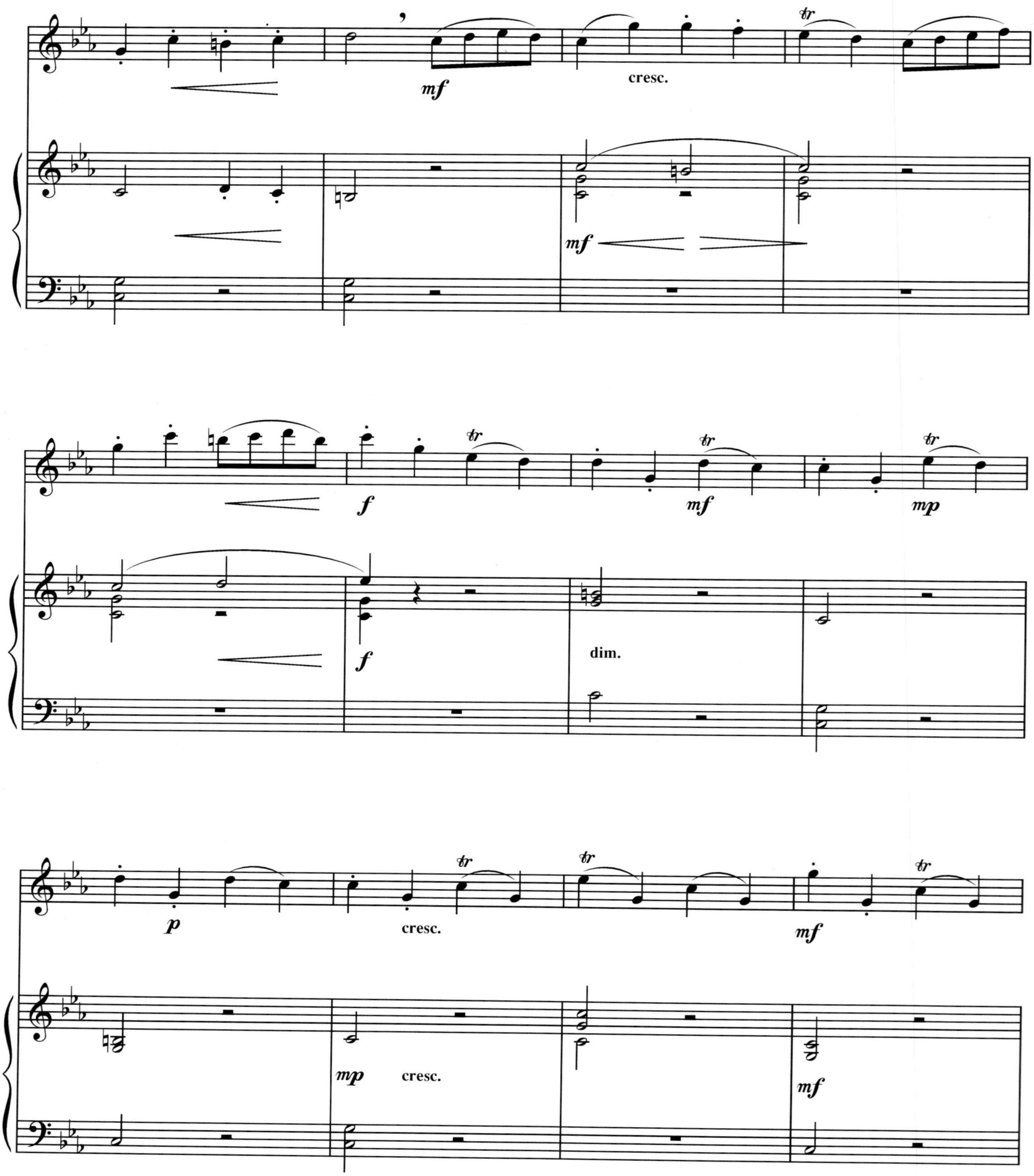
mf
cresc.
tr
mf
f
tr
mf
mp
dim.
p
cresc.
mp
cresc.
mf

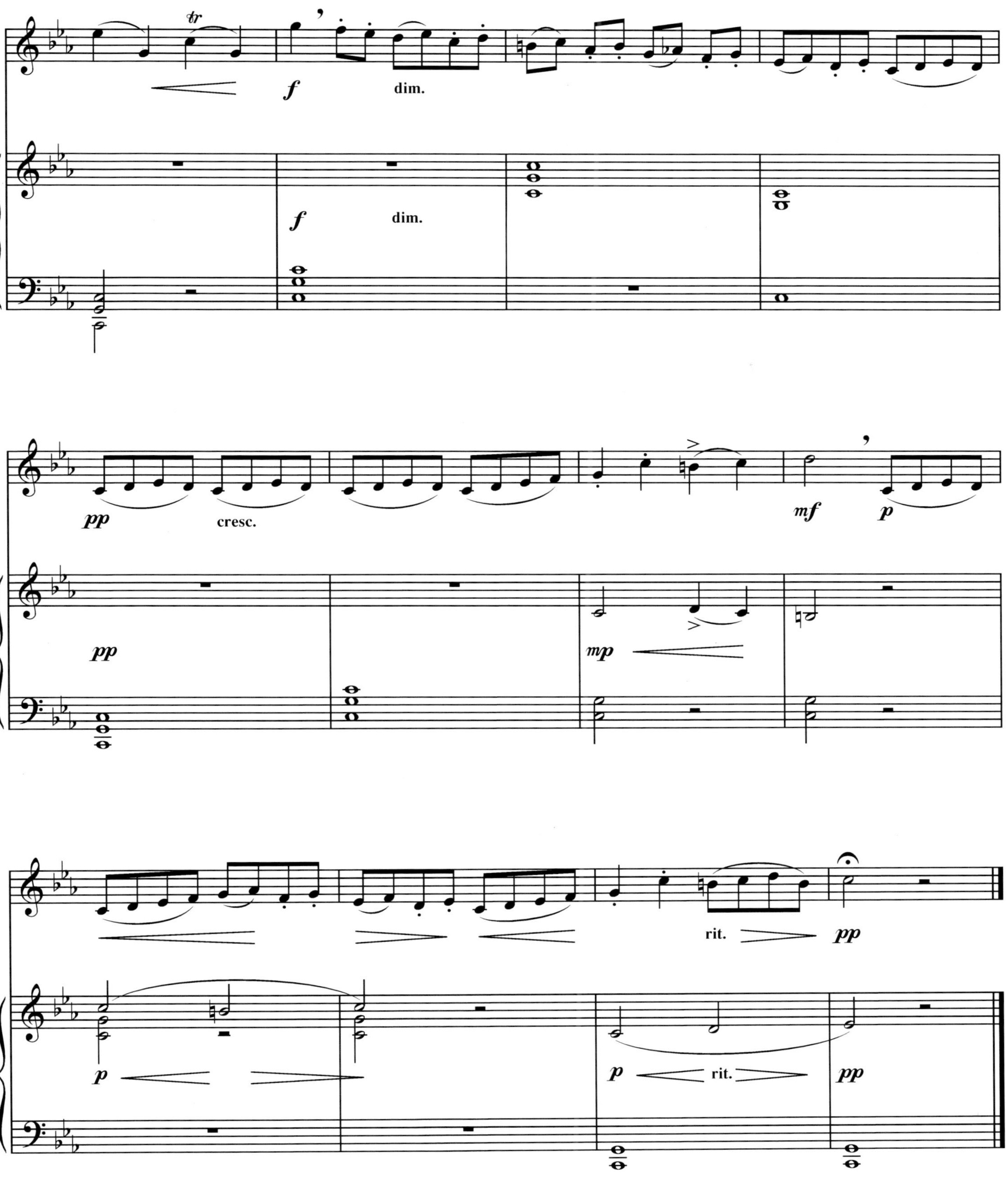
tr
f
dim.
f
dim.
pp
cresc.
mf
p
pp
mp
rit.
pp
p
p
rit.
pp

Care e Dolce

(Somewhat Sweetly)

Alessandro Scarlatti
(1659-1725)

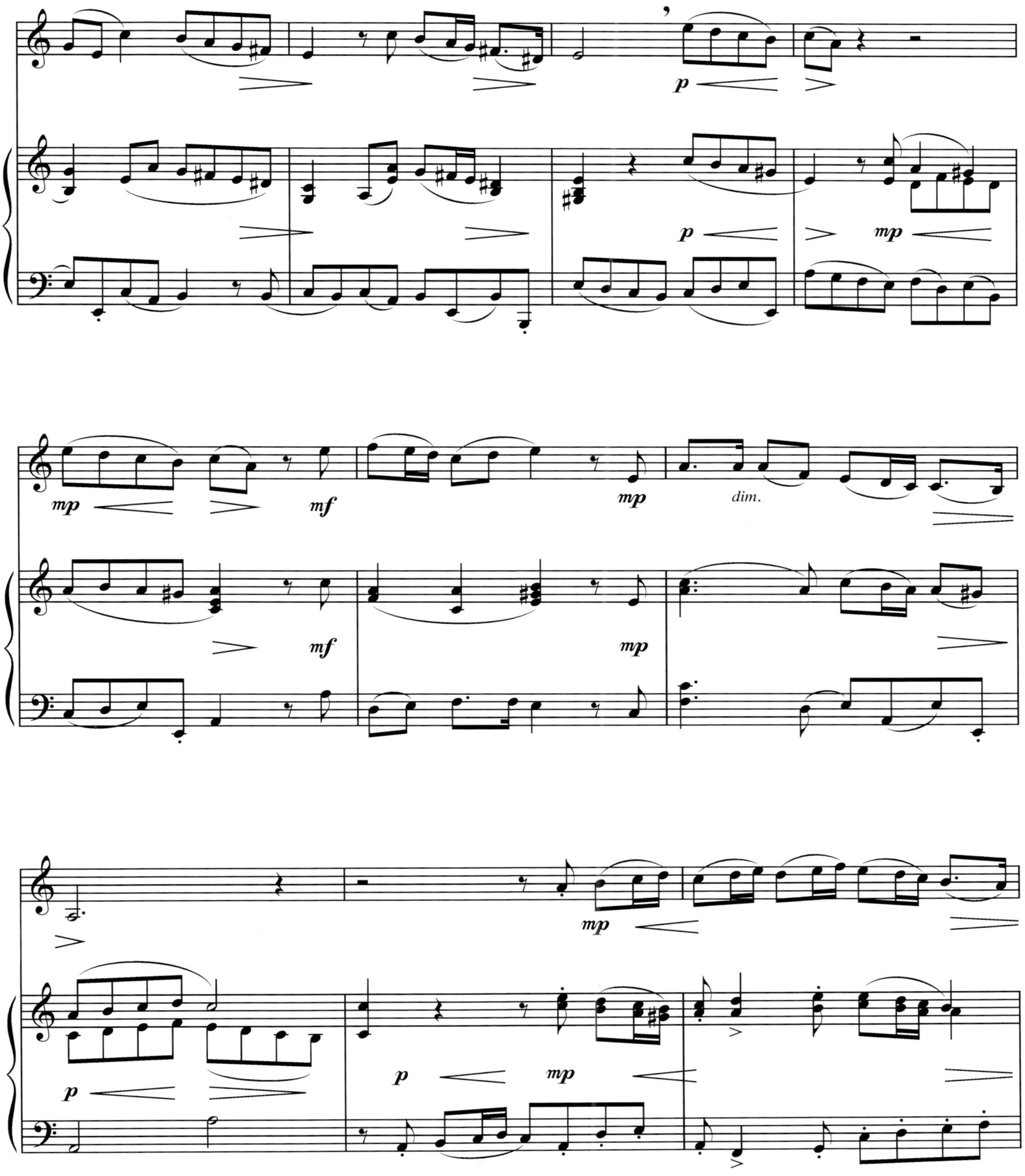
dim.

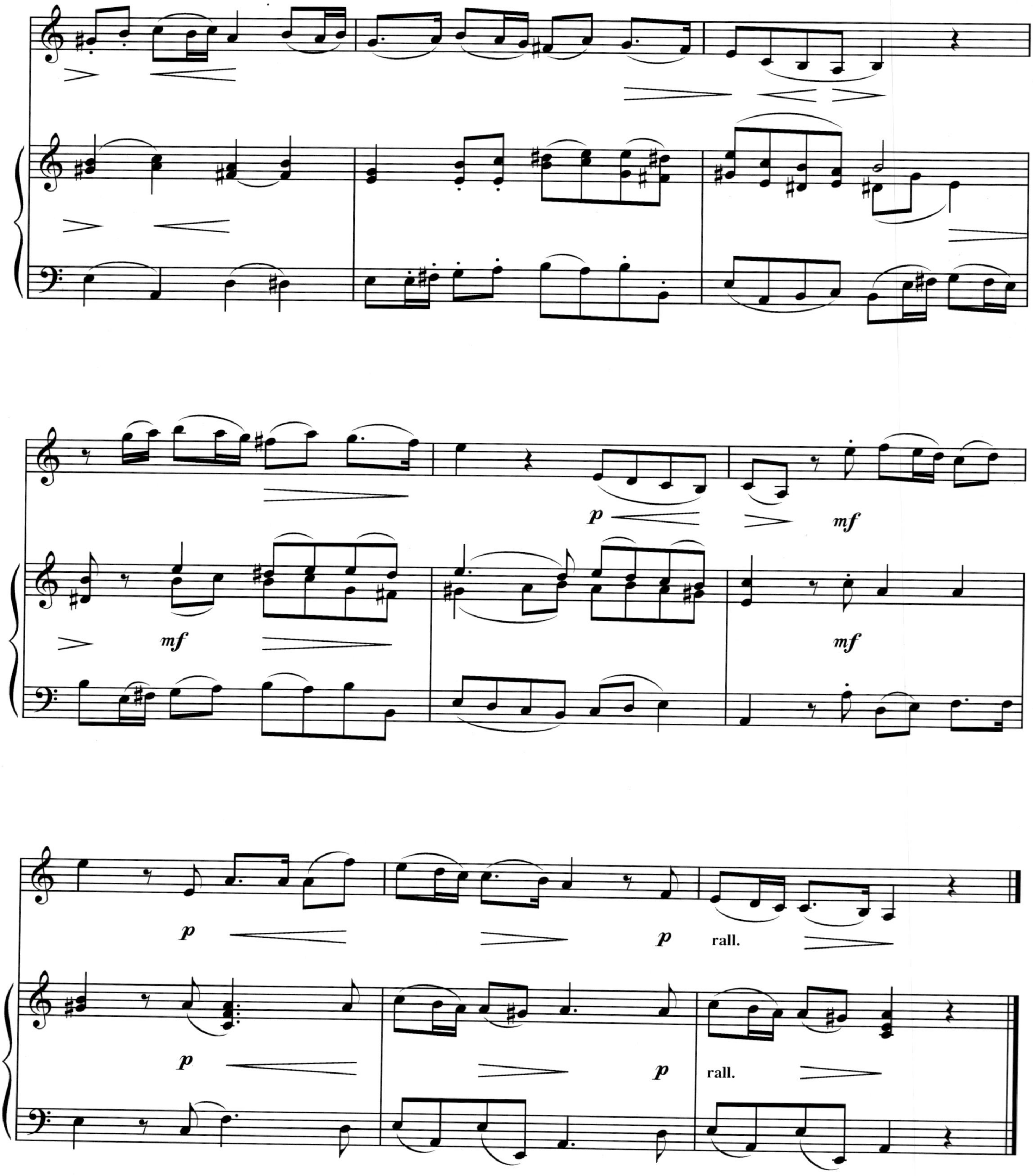
p
mf
mf
mf
p
p
rall.
p
p
rall.

Arietta

Alessandro Scarlatti

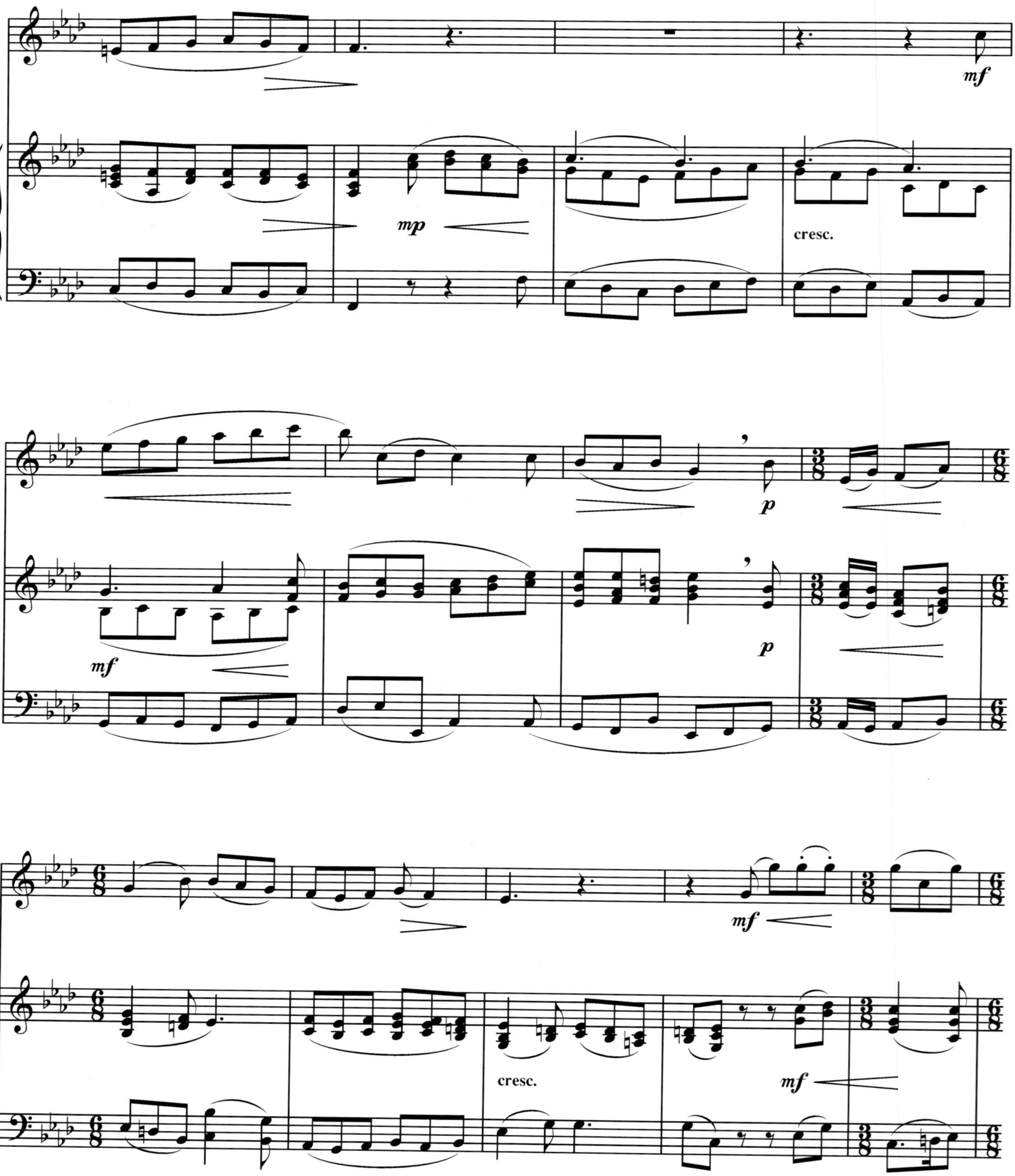
mf
mp
cresc.
p
p
mf
cresc.
mf
mf

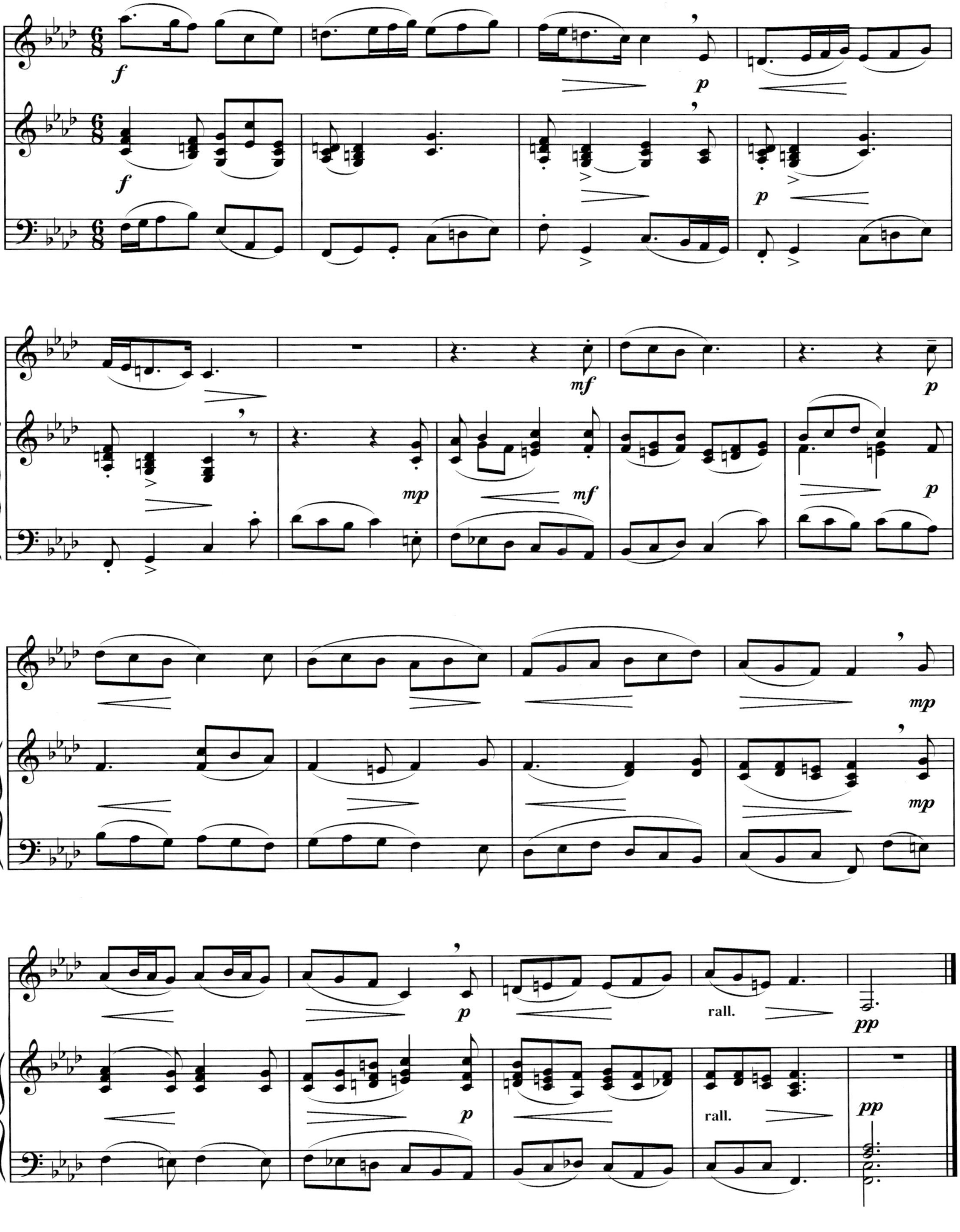
rall.
rall.

Minuet

Johann S. Bach
(1685-1750)

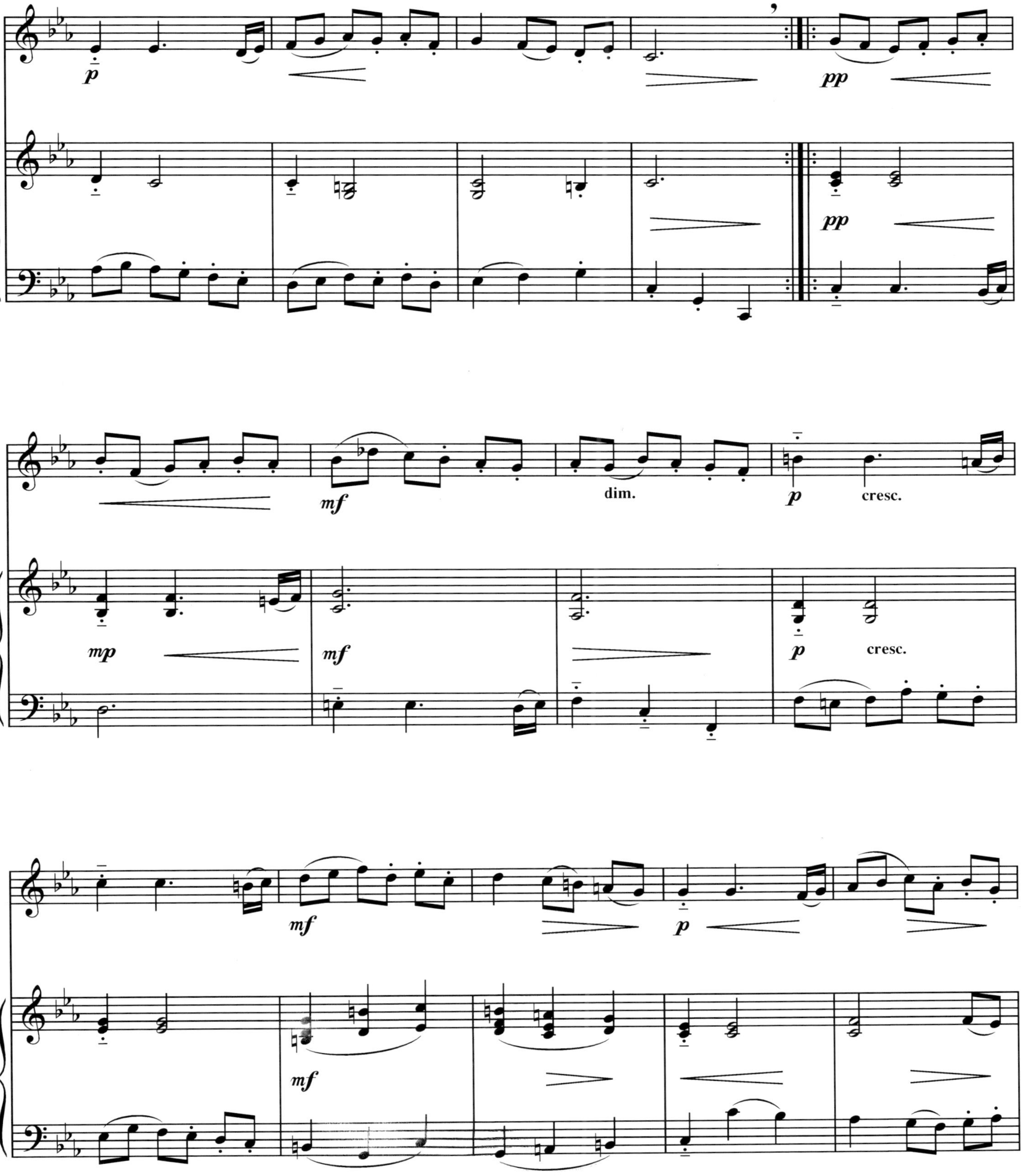
p
pp
mp
mf
dim.
cresc.

mp
mp
dim.
p
pp
pp
cresc.
p
cresc.
mp
mp
mf
mf
rit. (2nd time)
rit. (2nd time)

Sarabande

Johann S. Bach

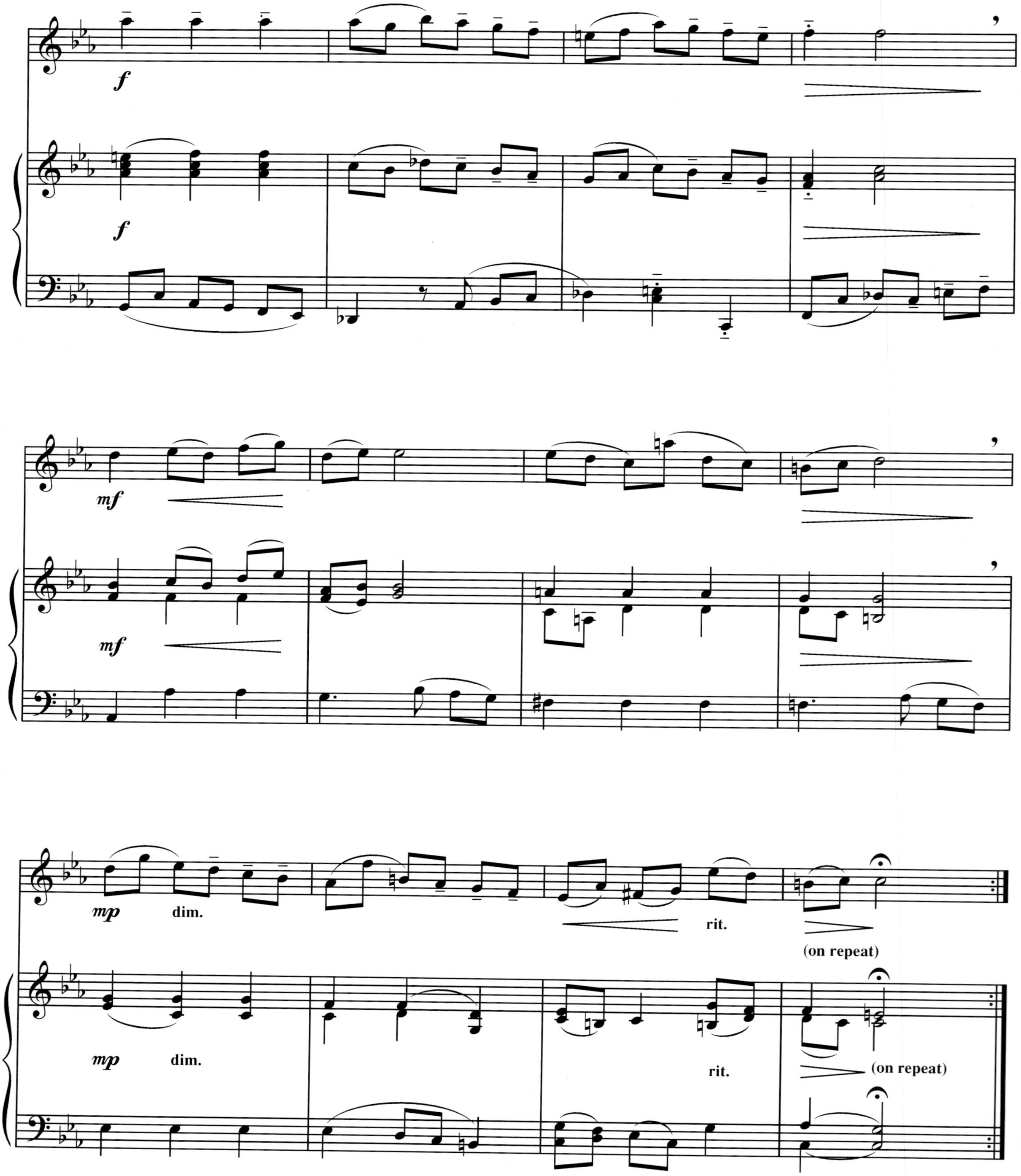
f
f
mf
mf
mp
dim.
rit.
(on repeat)
mp
dim.
rit.
(on repeat)

Air from the Messiah

G. F. Handel
(1685-1759)

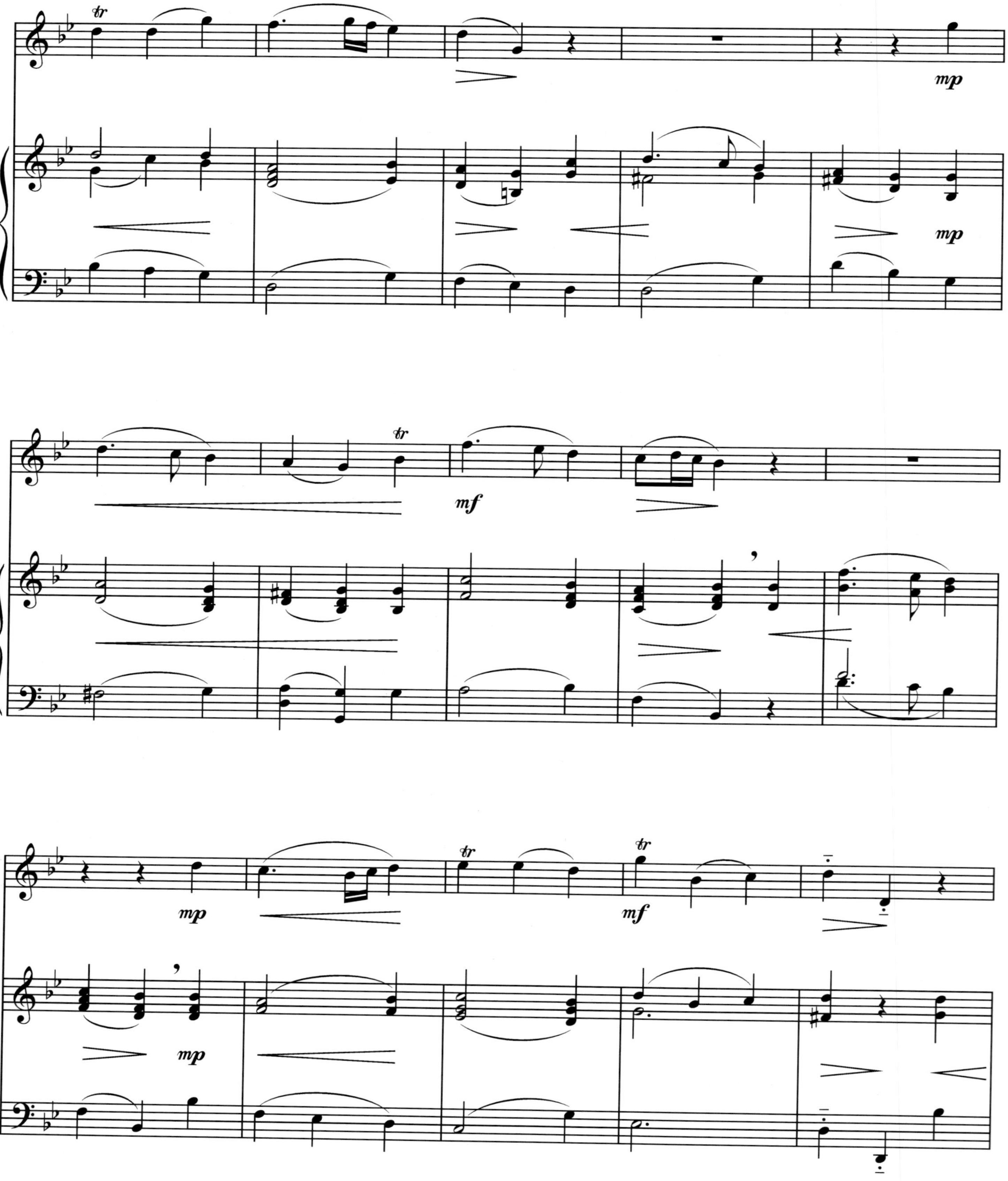
tr
mp
mp
mf
mp
mp
mf

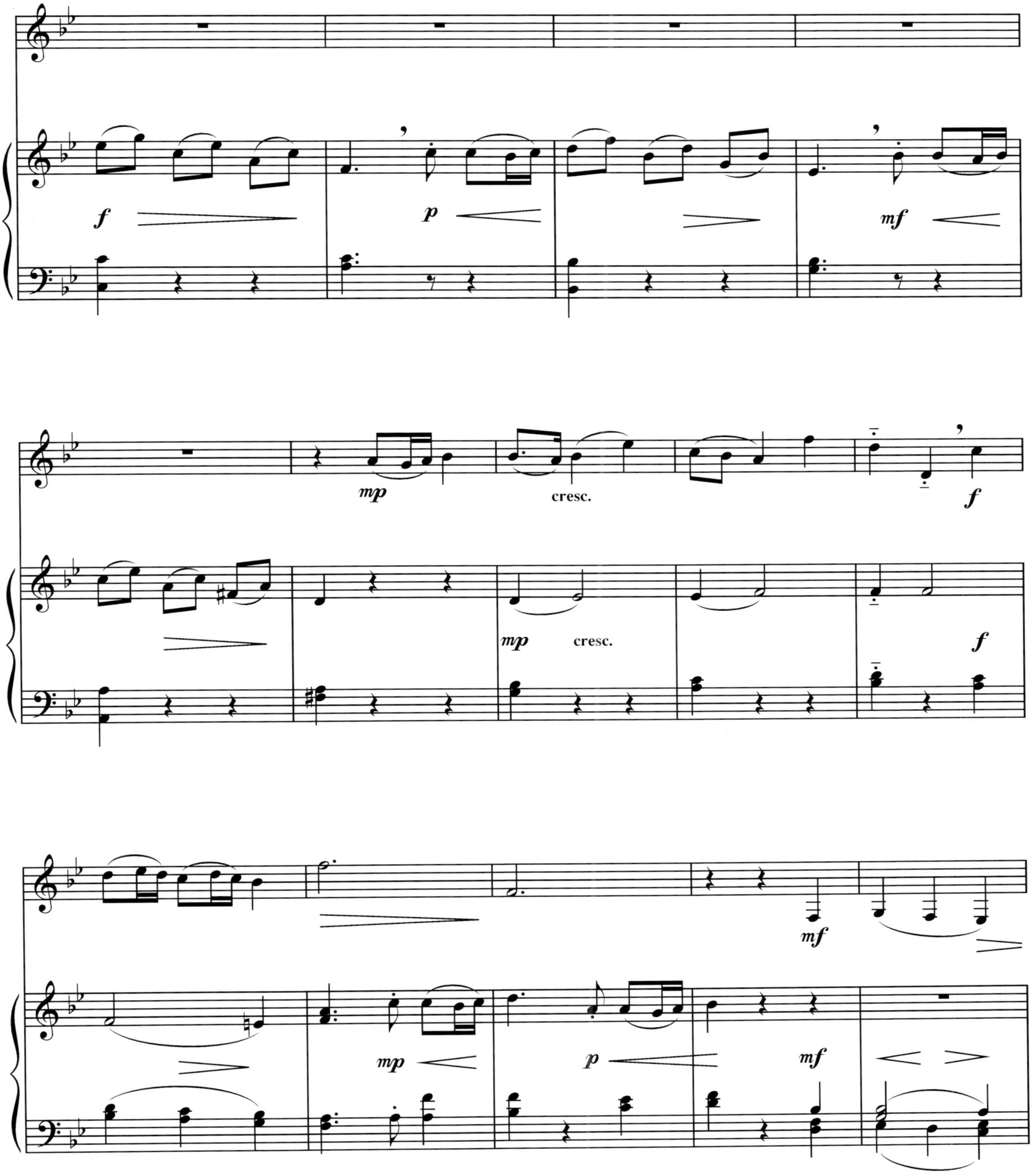
cresc.
cresc.

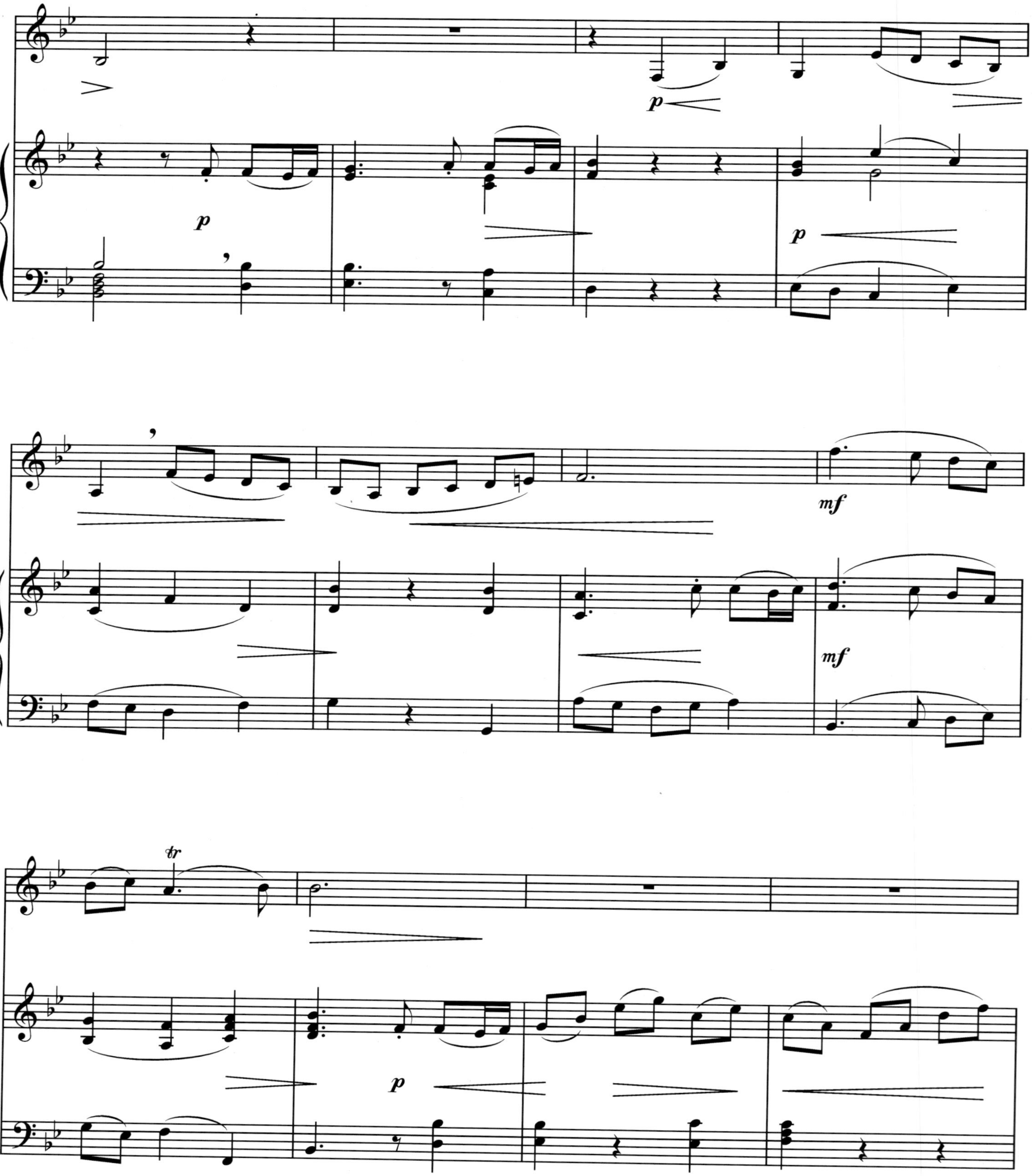
p
p
p
mf
mf
tr
p

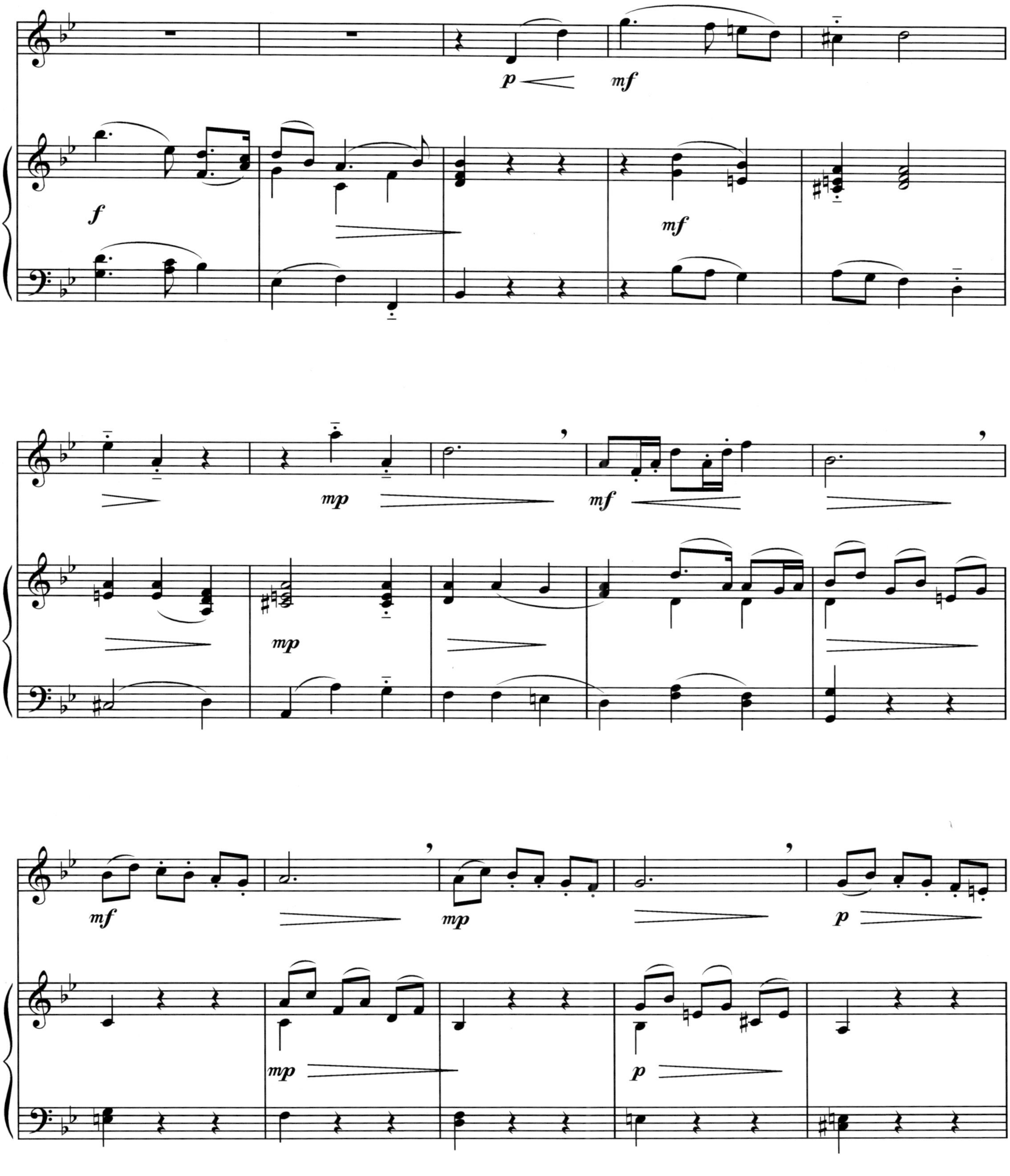
p
mf
f
mf
mp
mp
mf
mf
mp
mp
p
p

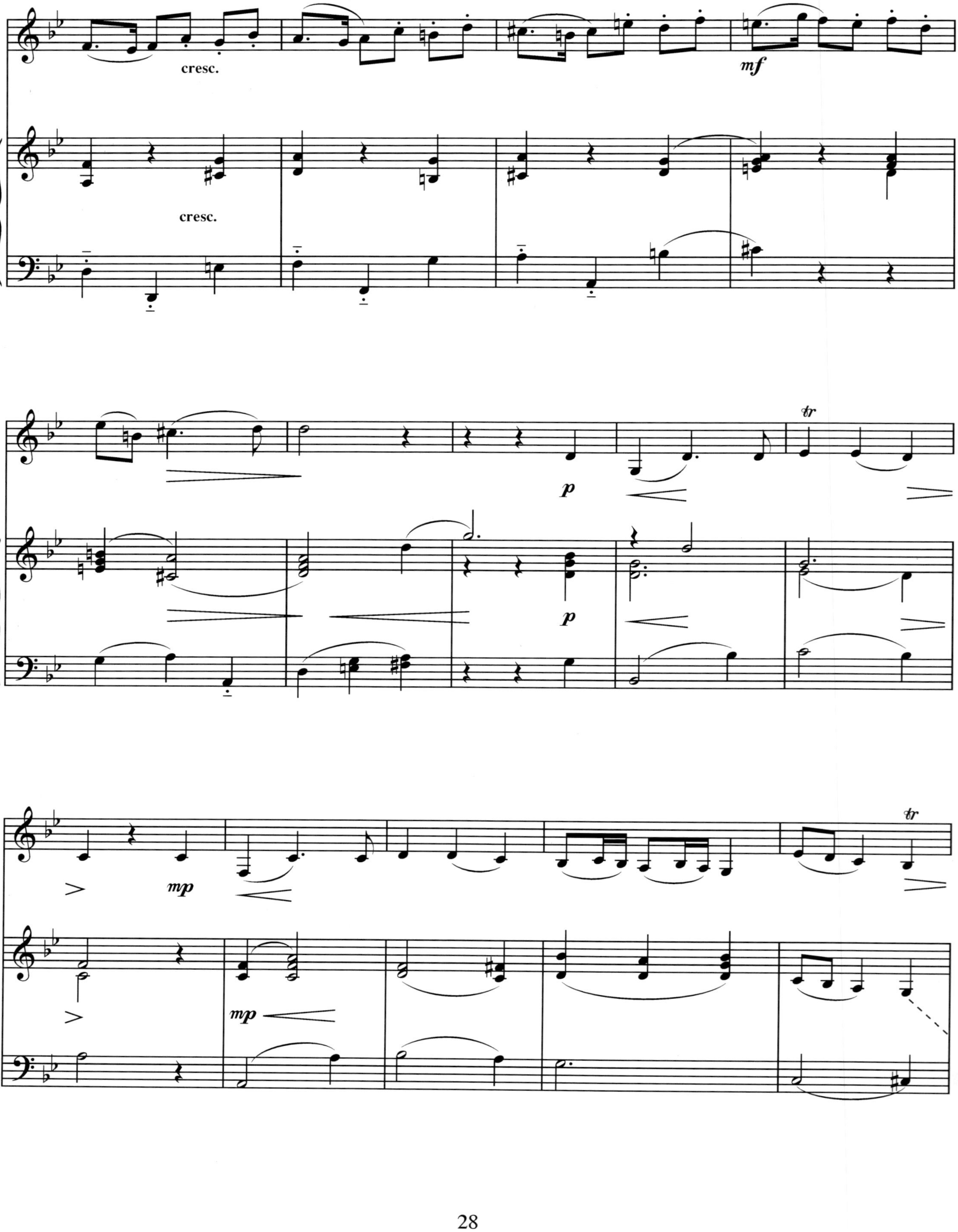
cresc.
mf
cresc.
tr
p
p
mp
tr
mp

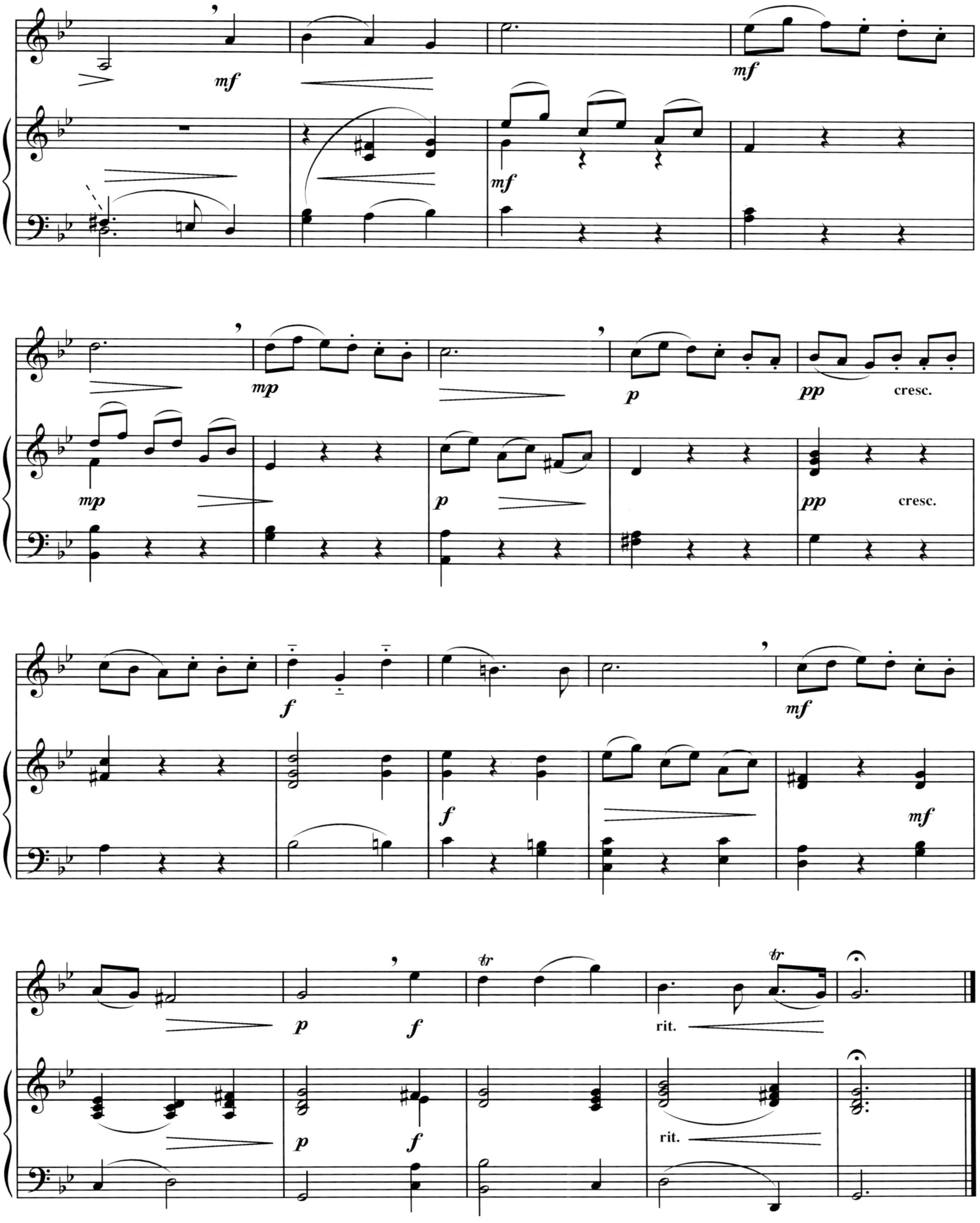
mf
mf
mf
mp
p
pp
cresc.
mp
p
pp
cresc.
f
mf
f
mf
p
f
rit.
p
f
rit.

Pastorale

Domenic Scarlatti
(1685-1757)

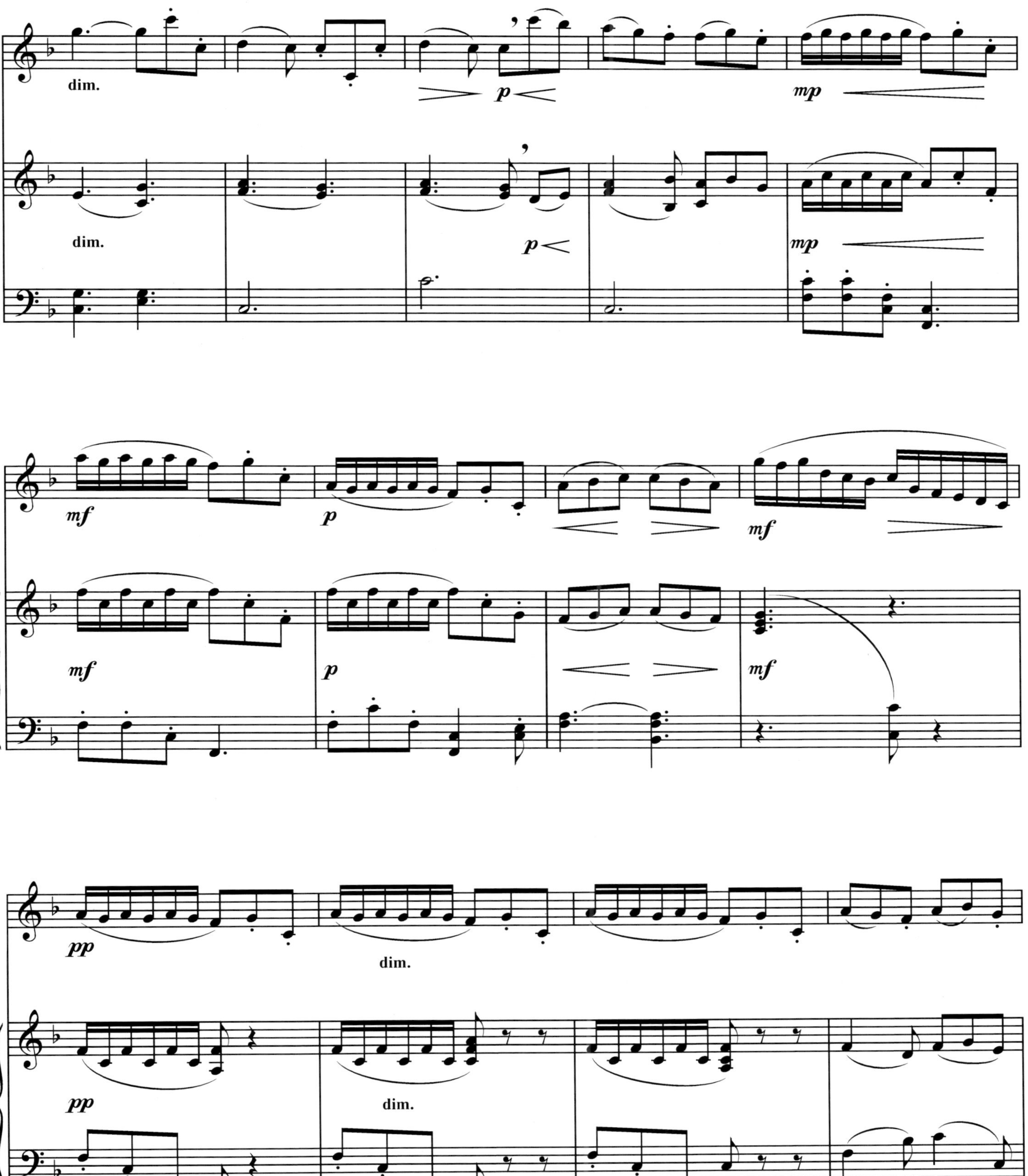
dim.
p
mp
dim.
p
mp
mf
p
mf
mf
p
mf
pp
dim.
pp
dim.

A tempo
f
rit.
mf
p
slen.
mf
f
rit.
mf
p
slen.
A tempo
pp
p
p
pp
p
p
cresc.
p
cresc.

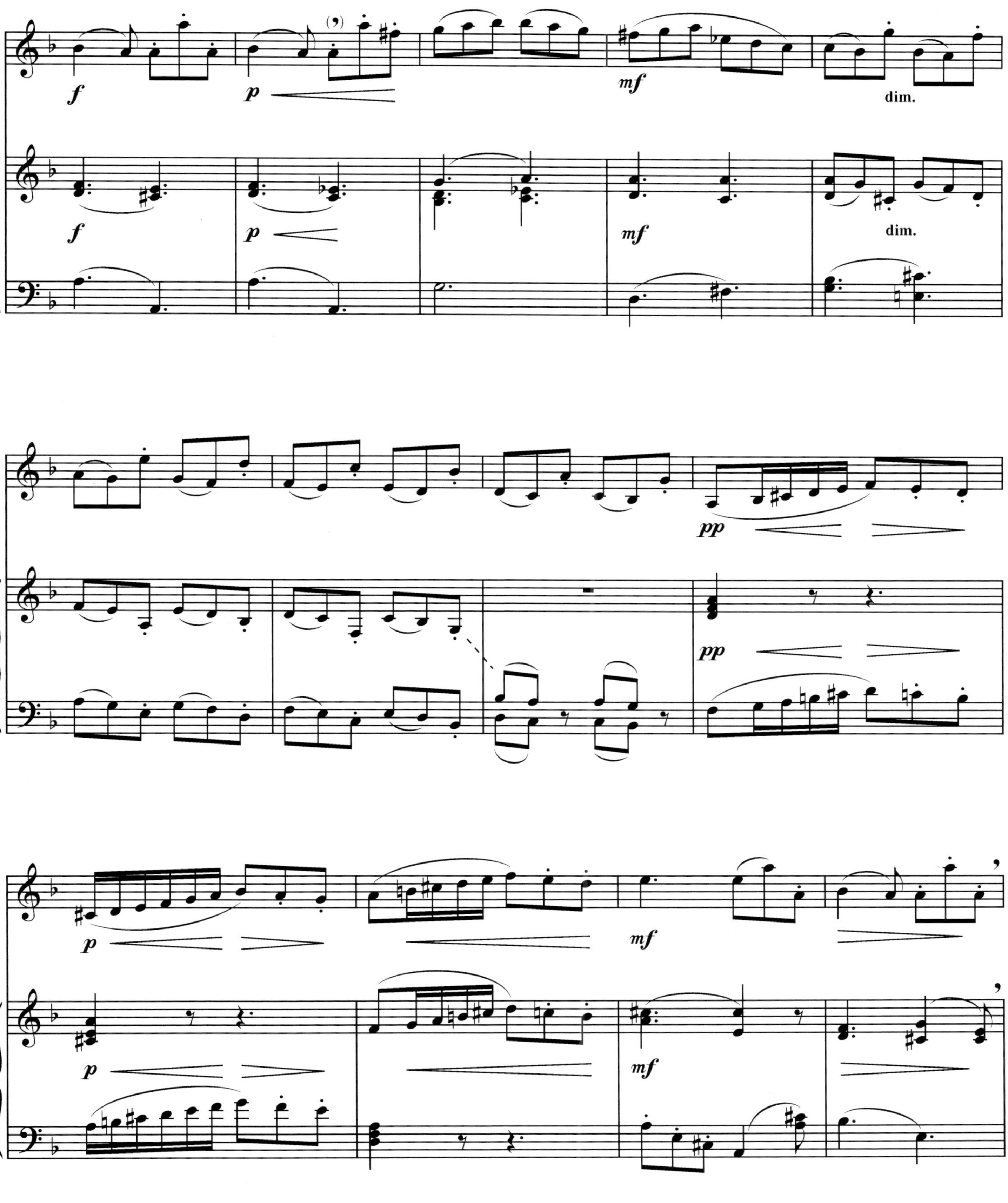
dim.
dim.

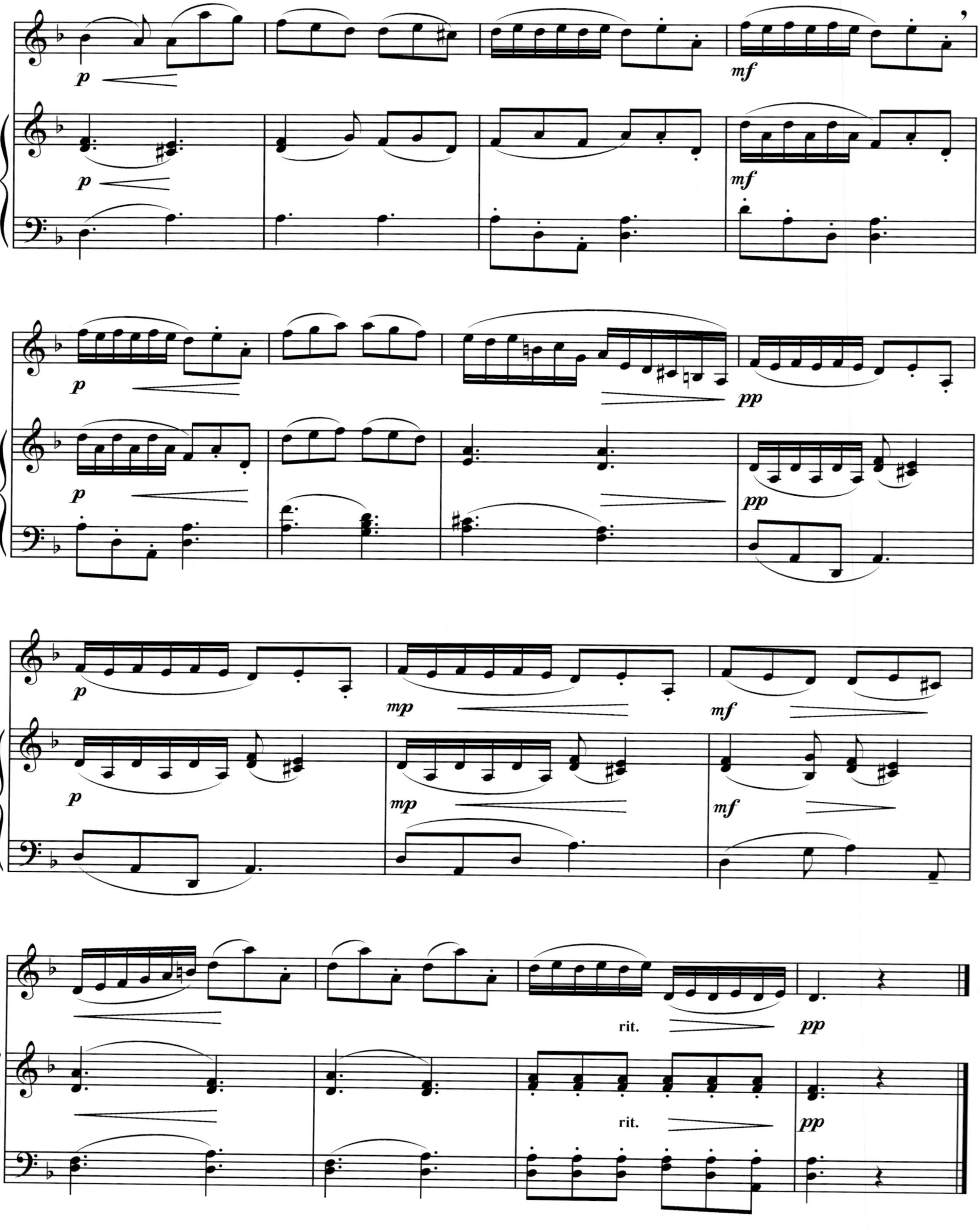
p
mf
p
pp
p
mp
mf
rit.
pp

Gavotte

Johann S. Bach
(1685-1750)

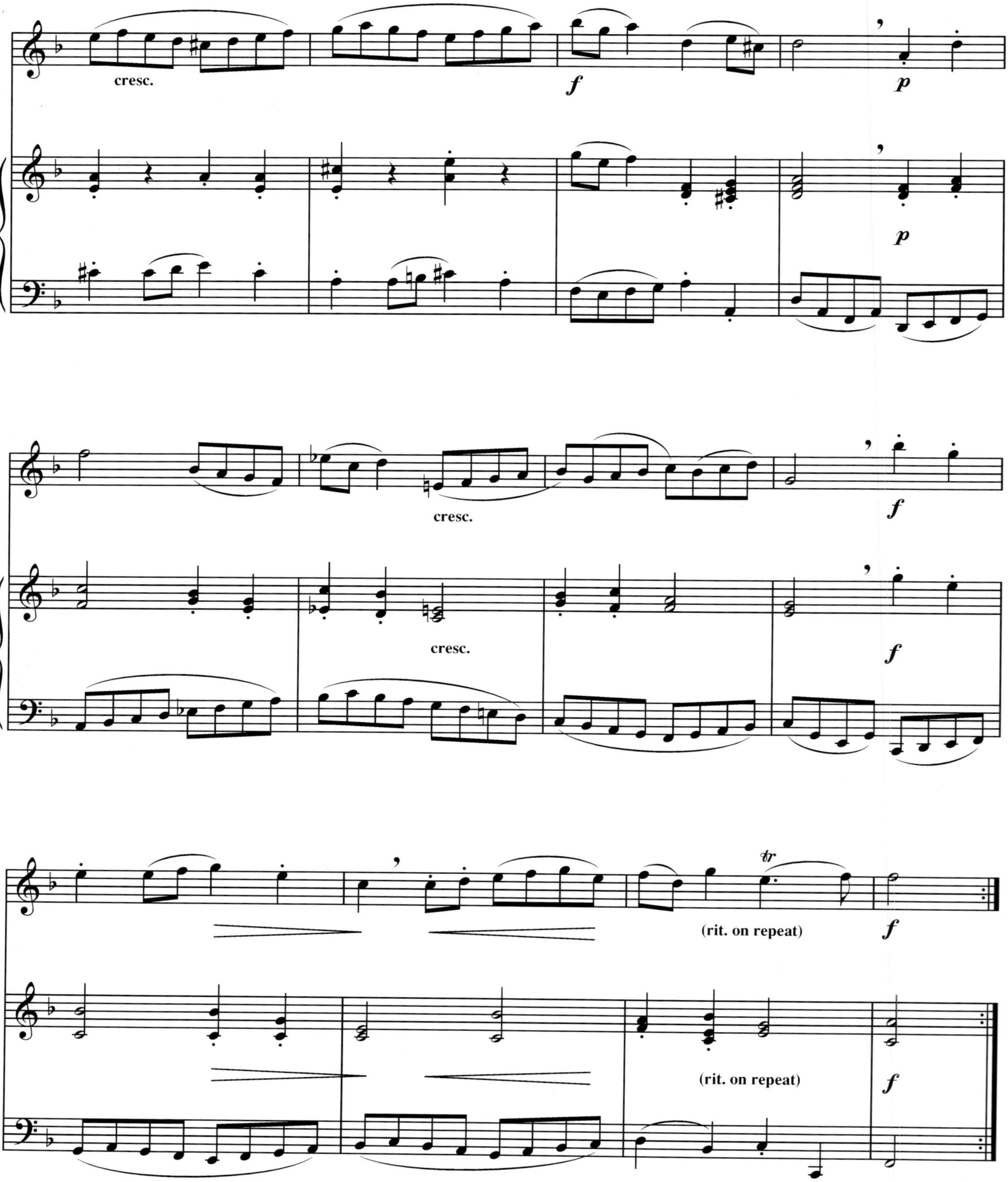
cresc.
cresc.
cresc.
(rit. on repeat)
(rit. on repeat)

Passacaglia

Antonio Vivaldi
(1680-1741)

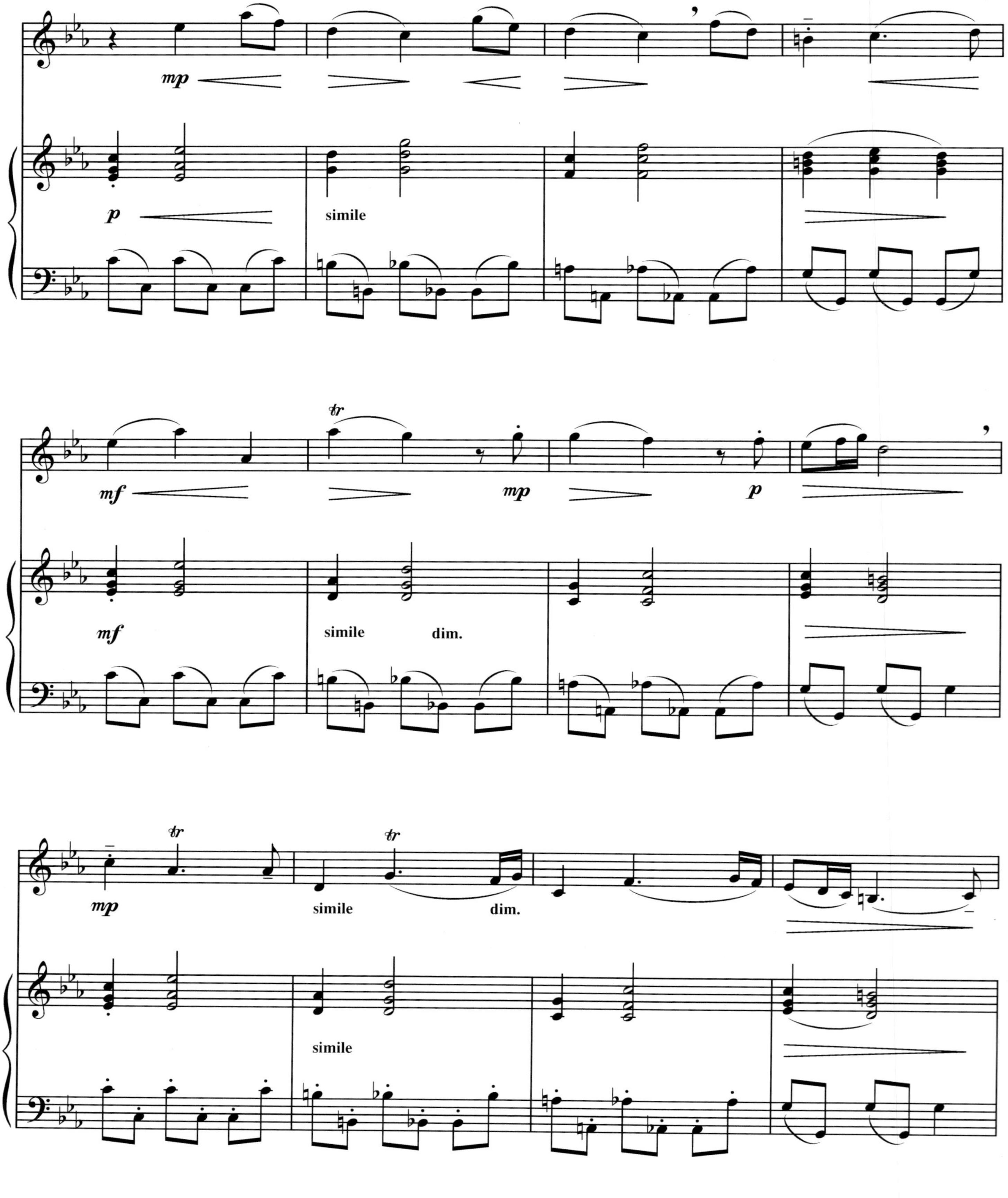
mp
p
simile
mf
simile
dim.
mp
p
mf
mp
simile
dim.
simile

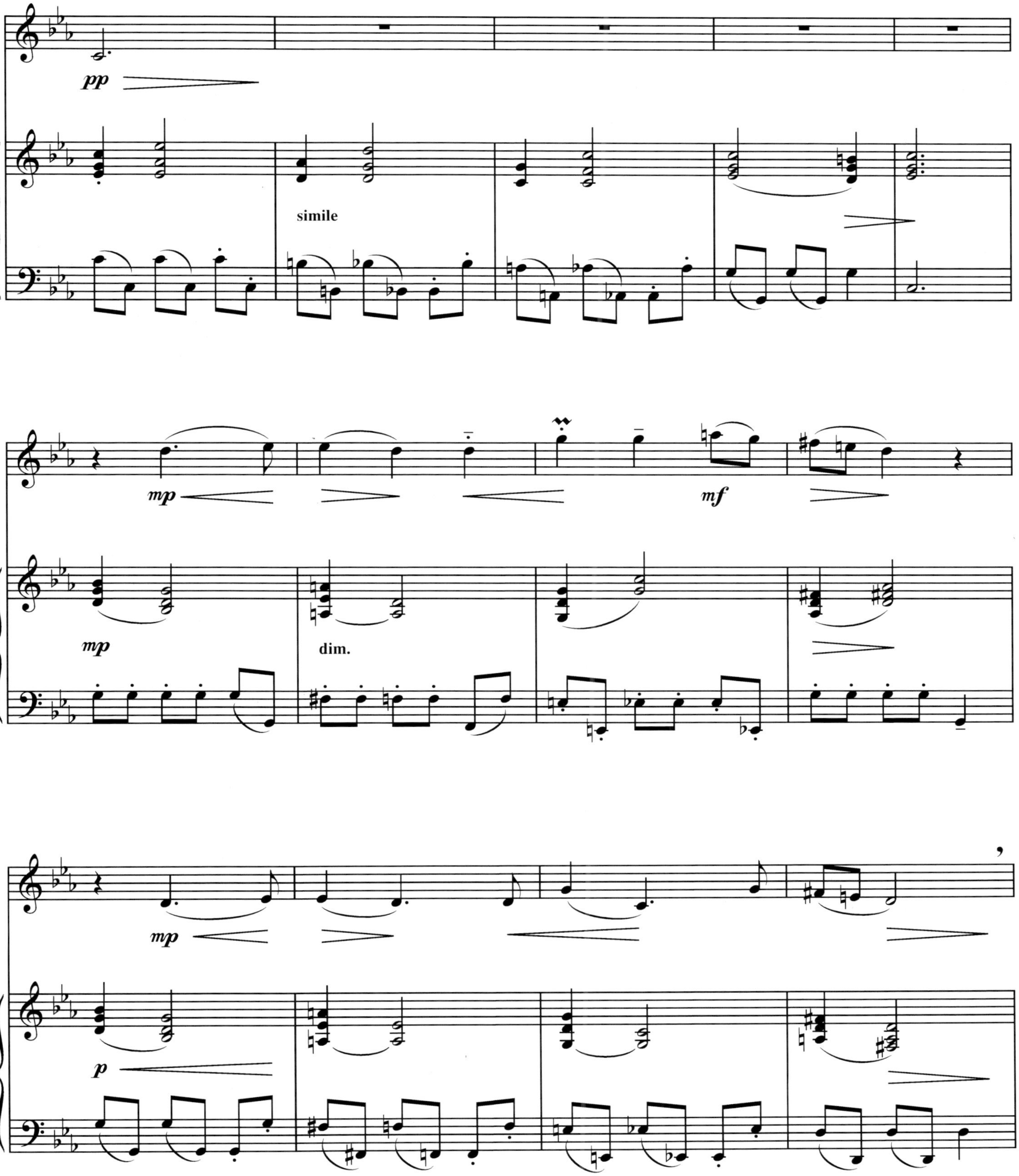
pp
simile
mp
mf
mp
dim.
mp
p

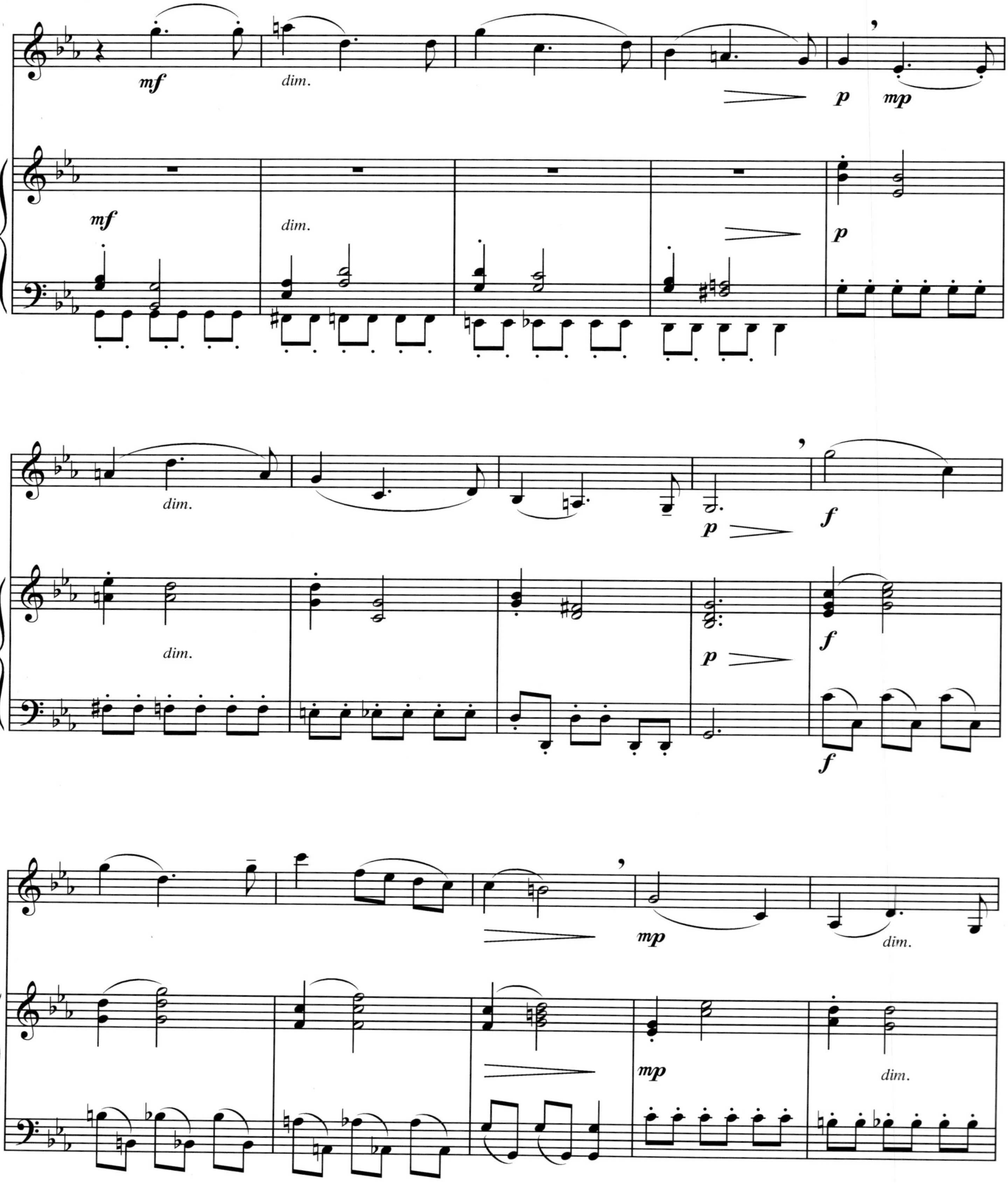
mf
dim.
p
mp
f

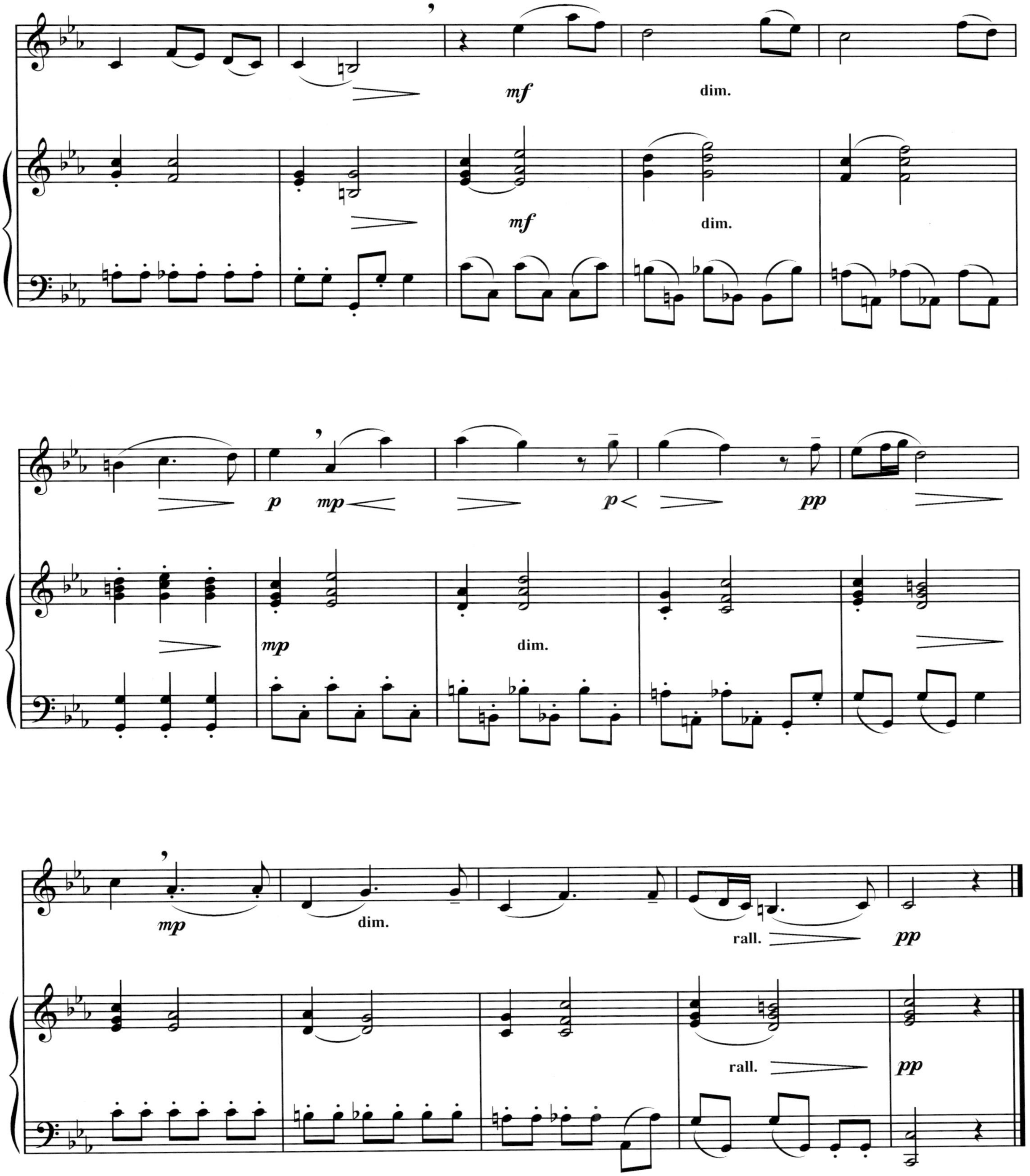
mf
dim.
mf
dim.
p
mp
p
pp
mp
dim.
mp
dim.
rall.
pp
rall.
pp

Andante from Sonata

C. P. E. Bach
(1714-1788)

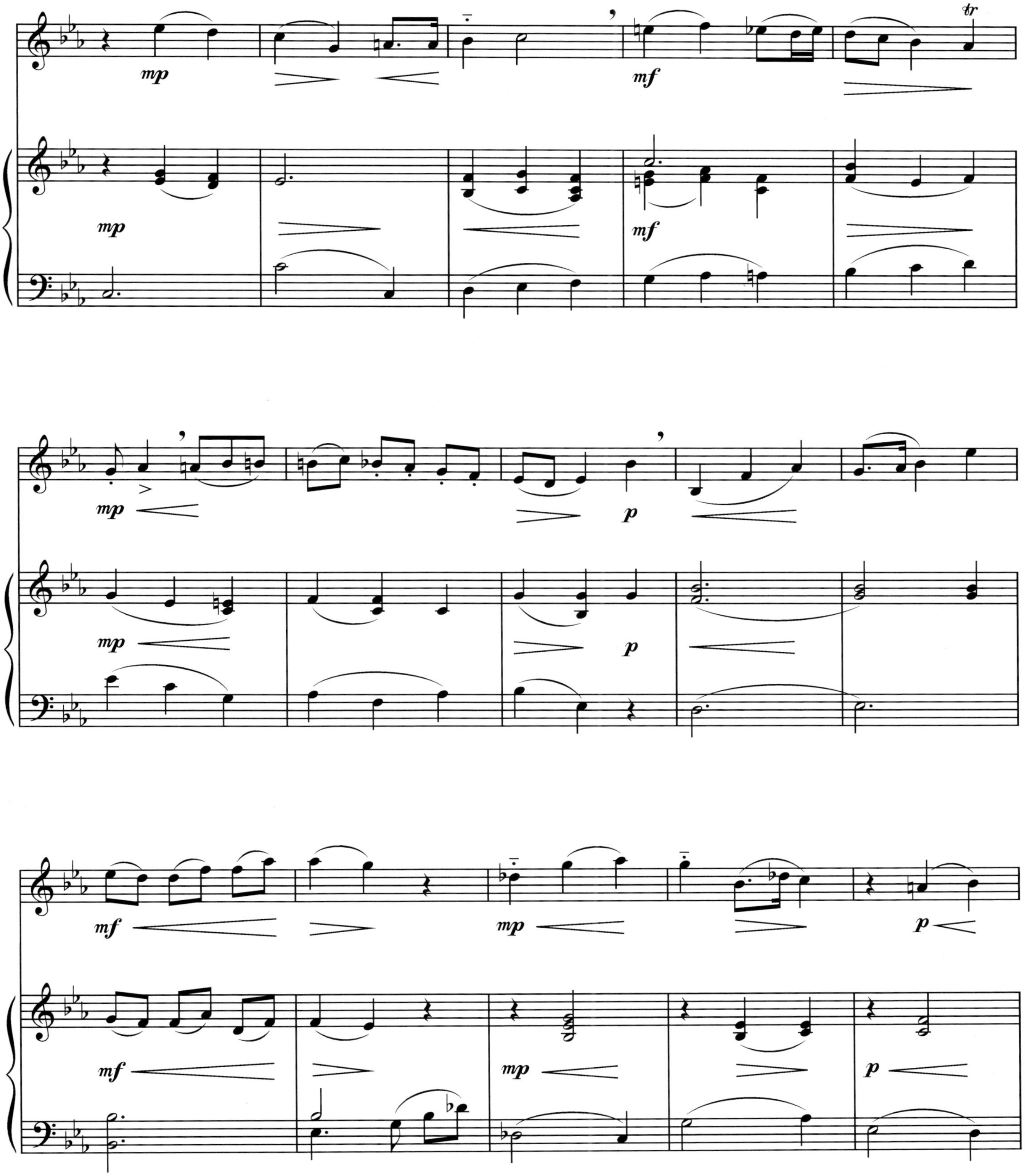
mp
mf
tr
mp
mf
p
mp
mf
mp
p

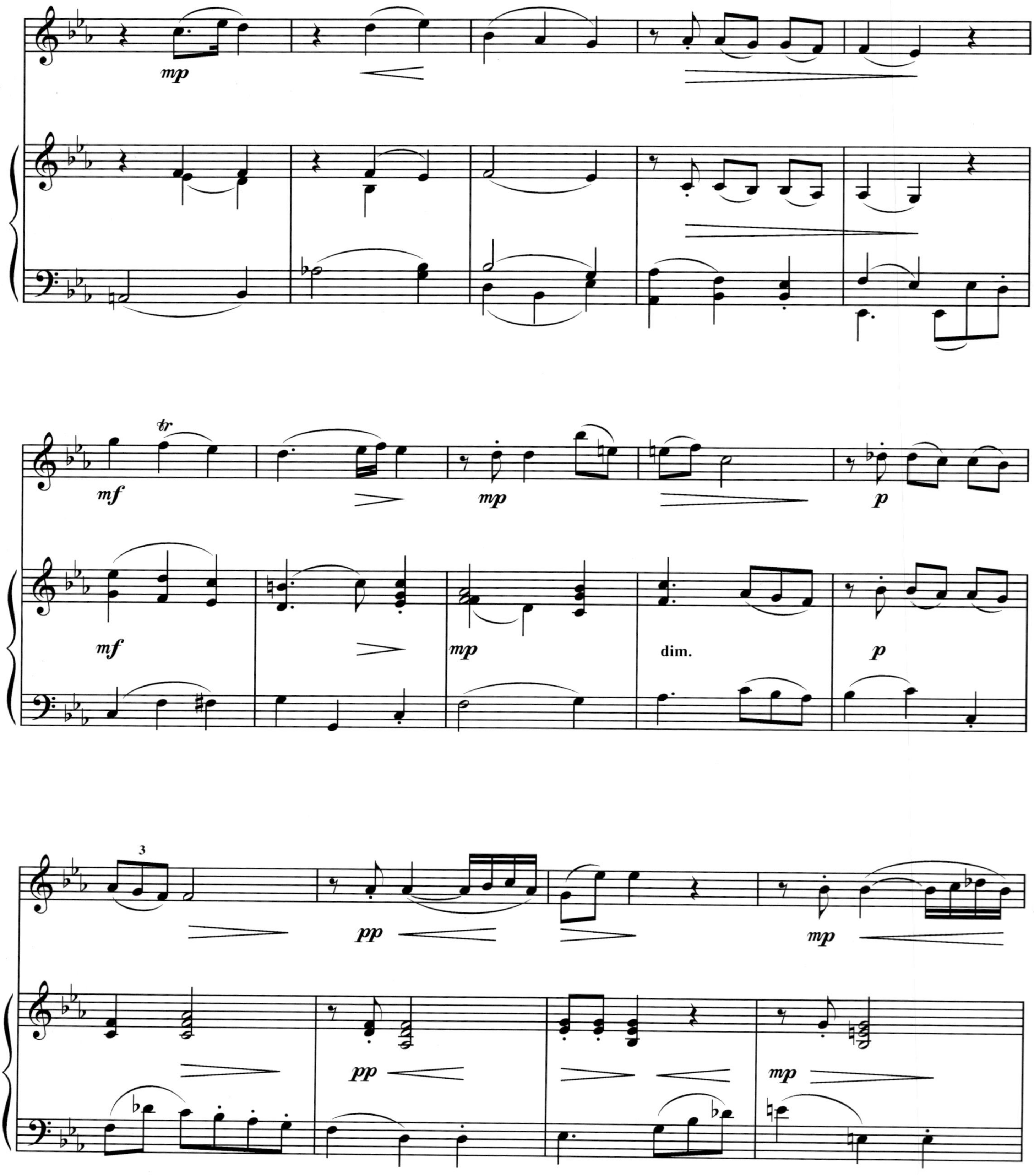
dim.

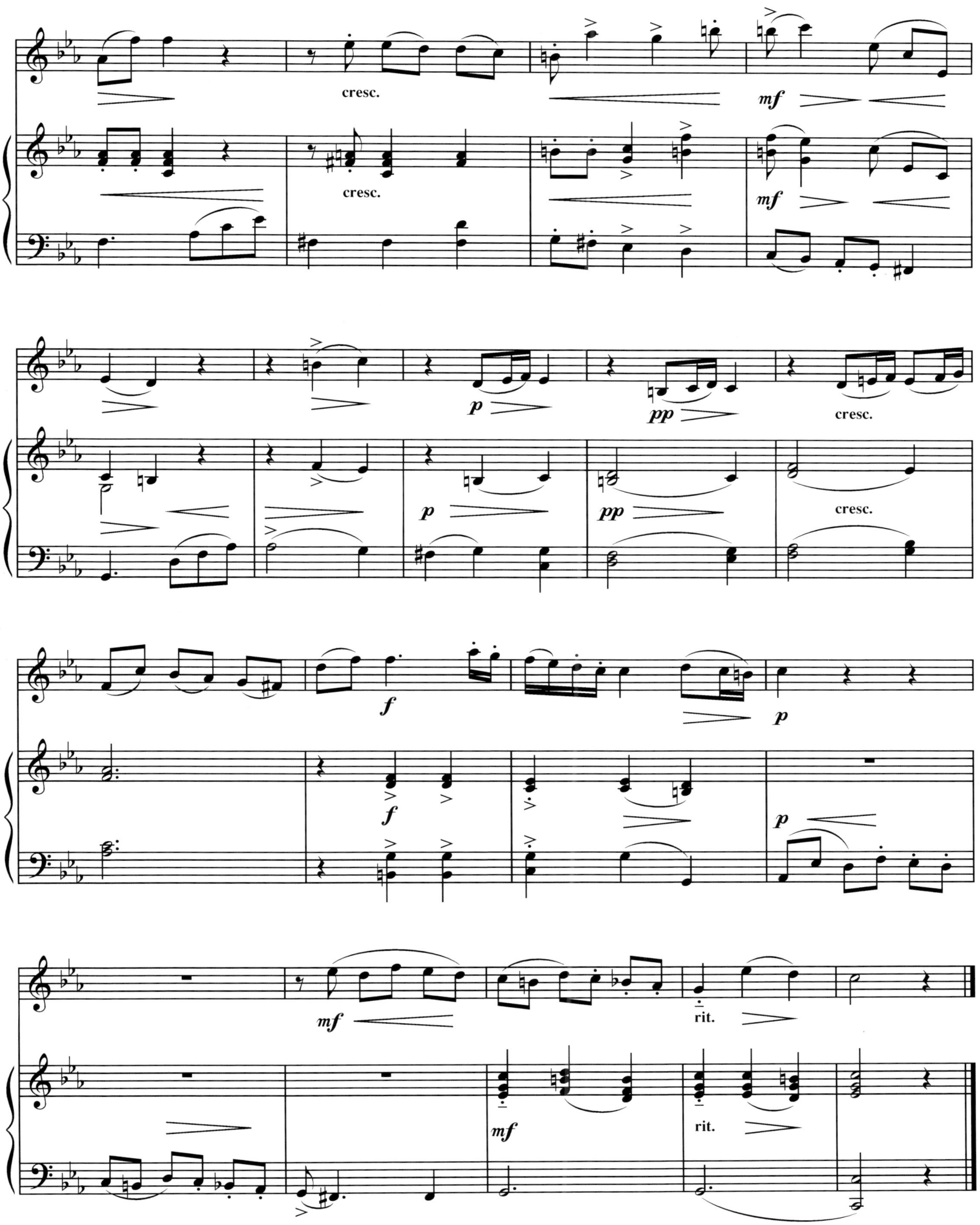
cresc.
cresc.
mf
mf
p
pp
cresc.
p
pp
cresc.
f
p
f
p
mf
rit.
mf
rit.

Allemande

Johann J. Froberger
(1616 -1667)

Courante

Johann J. Froberger

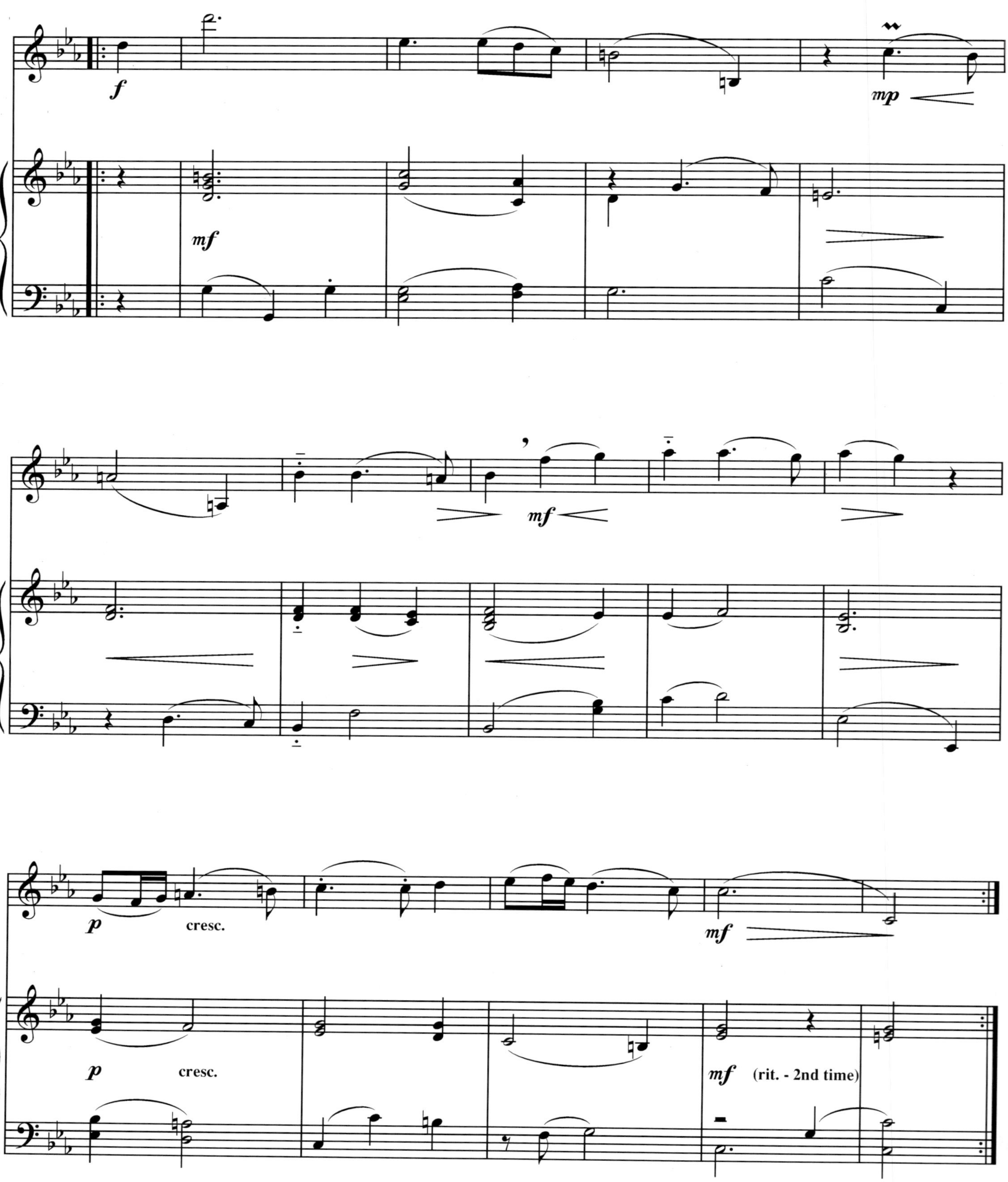
f
mp
mf
mf
mf
p
cresc.
mf
p
cresc.
mf
(rit. - 2nd time)

Sarabande

Johann J. Froberger

Gigue

Johann J. Froberger

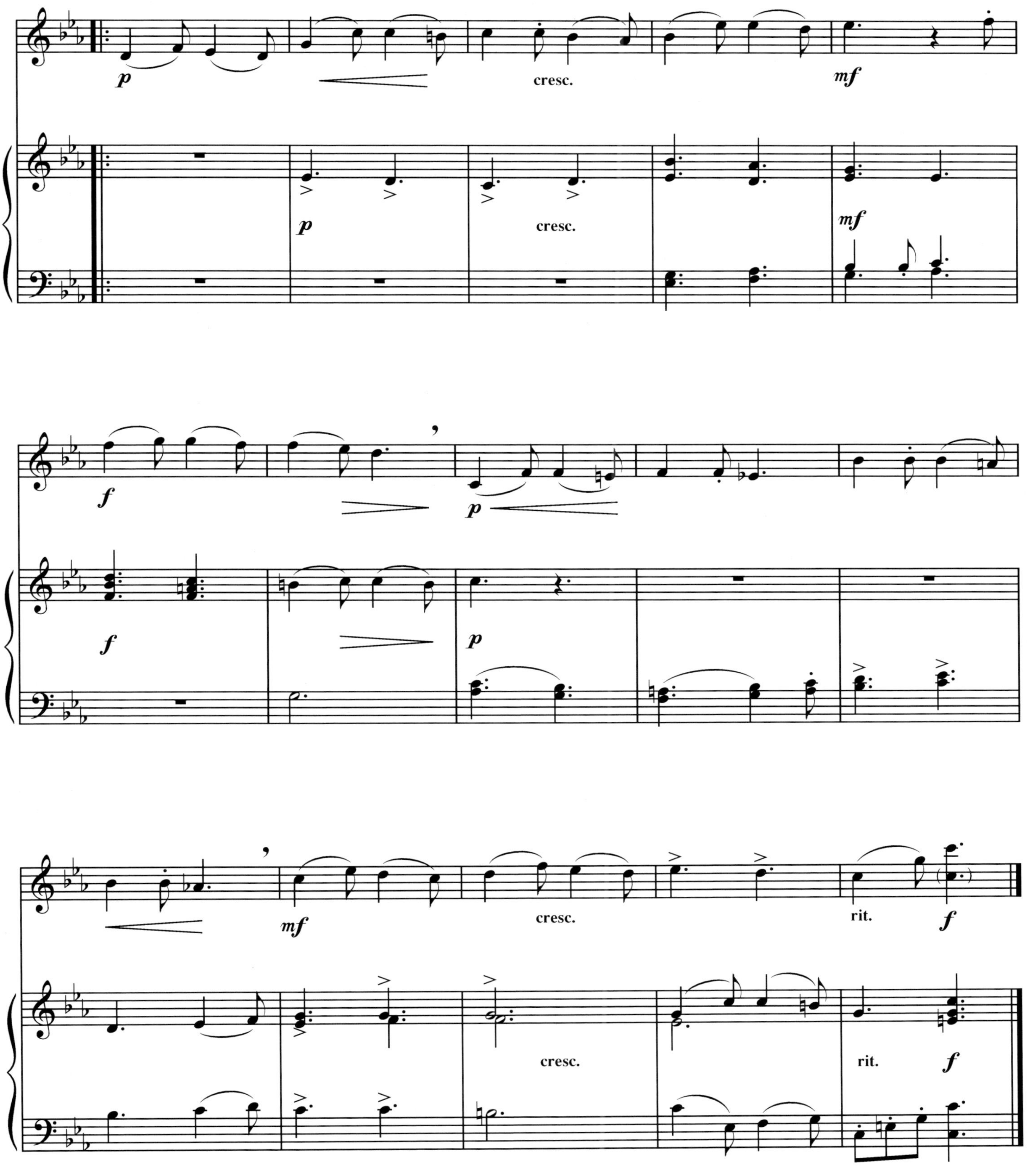
p
cresc.
mf
f
rit.

Other Mel Bay Clarinet Books

Complete Jazz Clarinet Book (W. Bay)

100 Essential Exercises for Clarinet (Elliott)

Clarinet Fingering Chart (W. Bay)

Clarinet Fingering and Scale Chart (Nelson)

Technical Development for the Clarinetist (Heim)

Tone, Technique & Staccato (Galper)

Upbeat Scales & Arpeggios (Galper)

Clarinet Solos on Balkan Folk Songs and Dances (Puscoiu)

Easy Klezmer Tunes (Phillips)

Klezmer Book (Galper)

20 Clarinet Duets from Baroque to the 20th Century (Heim)

25 Solos for Clarinet from the Unaccompanied Works of J. S. Bach (Leonard)

Classical Repertoire for Clarinet Vol. 1 (Puscoiu)

Favorite Student Clarinet Classics (W. Bay)

Laurindo Almeida: Duets for Clarinet and Guitar

Mozart for Clarinet (Heim)

Music of Brahms for Clarinet (Heim)

Recital Pieces for Clarinet from the Period of Impressionism (Heim)

Solo Pieces for the Beginning Clarinetist (Heim)

Solo Pieces for the Intermediate Clarinetist (Heim)

Solo Pieces for the Advanced Clarinetist (Heim)

101 Easy Songs for Clarinet (Maroni)

Beginning Clarinetist's Songbook (Maroni)

Easy Classics for Clarinet with Piano Accompaniment (Spitzer)

Easy Duets for Clarinet (Puscoiu)

Fun with the Clarinet (W. Bay)

More Fun with the Clarinet (W. Bay)

Christmas Solos for Beginning Clarinet Level 1 (Heim)

Instrumental Caroling Book (W. Bay)

My Very Best Christmas: Clarinet (Khanagov)

Sacred Melodies for Clarinet Solo (Heim)

WWW.MELBAY.COM